The History of Scotland

History Nerds

Published by History Nerds, 2022.

While every precaution has been taken in the preparation of this book, the publisher assumes no responsibility for errors or omissions, or for damages resulting from the use of the information contained herein.

THE HISTORY OF SCOTLAND

First edition. April 12, 2022.

ISBN: 979-8215891001

Written by History Nerds.

Also by History Nerds

Celtic History
Ireland

Great Wars of the World
World War 1
World War 2
The Napoleonic Wars: One Shot at Glory
The Serbian Revolution: 1804-1835
Peace Won by the Saber: The Crimean War, 1853-1856
The Wars of the Roses

Irish Heroes
Grace O'Malley: The Pirate Queen of Ireland
William Butler Yeats: Nobel Prize Winning Poet
Scáthach
Finn McCool

The History of the Vikings

Vikings
Longships on Restless Seas

The Rise and Fall of Empires
Rome: The Rise and Fall

Standalone
The History of the United Kingdom
The History of Ireland
The History of America
Stalin
The Fiery Maelstrom of Freedom
The History of Scotland
Robert the Bruce
William Wallace: Scotland's Great Freedom Fighter
The History of Wales

Table of Contents

The History of Scotland:
To the Windswept Shores of Alba
Introduction

Through the glens and along the lochs, beyond forests and windswept isles, the Scottish people endured the many tests of time. The proud nation of Scotland definitely has plenty to boast about: its history is long and tumultuous, filled with a fight for freedom and undefeatable Gaelic identity. From mankind's earliest footsteps to the dawn of ethnicities, and all the way to the great migrations of nomads - the mountainous landscapes of Scotland were slowly shaped into a distinct nation that we know and love today. It was a rocky road, without a doubt: the Scottish people are admired for their strong love of freedom and their very long struggle to attain it.

For many centuries, Scotland has been at the crossroads of history. Always fought over by greater powers, this wild land of tradition and heritage has been at the center of a historic whirlwind of war, conquest, and conflict. And in spite of it all, the Scottish people fiercely clung to their identity, pulling it with them through the ages.

But above all, this nation's history is without a doubt *colorful*. It is so diverse and exciting, like an archeological sandwich whose many layers you can peel off for years and years. For historians - and anyone who is enthusiastic about the world's past - Scotland is a real uncut gem. A diamond just waiting to be polished and displayed to the world in all its glory.

In this book we will uncover all these historic layers that comprise Scotland today. From the early inhabitants to the emergence of a Gaelic identity and the tumultuous Roman times of Classical Antiquity. We will dive into the turbulent Medieval period in Scotland, which greatly shaped the nation's future as we know it today. We will take a critical sideline glimpse into the constant friction with the English, and a complicated relationship with the Vikings and the Norse. We'll travel to the Hebrides, the Orkneys and the Shetland isles, studying their enigmatic identities torn between the Scottish and the Norse. And above all, we will try to piece together the puzzles of history as we uncover the true, unbiased, and ultimately *original* Scottish identity. This is the history of Scotland - in an exciting, brand-new light.

A Fast-Changing History:
The Roman and Early Medieval Ages in Scotland

The Ancient Romans were the focal point of classical antiquity - a powerful city-state that quickly rose to power over its neighbors, emerging as a strong and far-reaching republic. After just a few centuries, Rome spread across Europe and the Mediterranean, its culture and language spreading as fast as wildfire. And, in time, the shadow of Rome was bound to reach the British Isles. This it did, eventually. But did it ever reach Scotland? Before we answer this question, we must delve a bit deeper into the peculiar conundrum of the identity of Scotland's early inhabitants. Who exactly did the Romans encounter in these wild lands?

Before the accounts of the Roman scholars, generals, and historiographers, not much was known about the "native", inhabitants of Scotland. Like the whole of the British Isles, this region too was somewhat of a "crossroads" of ancient peoples. The turbulent currents of the sea always brought new migrants onto Scottish shores. Not all of them came to bring war and plunder - some simply settled and mixed with the peoples already living there. Over the many centuries, a unique identity was formed. Still, the region of modern Scotland was, for the most part, not isolated from the rest of the British Isles, and shared its fate with Ireland, Wales, and England. During the mid and late Bronze Age, for example, new technologies and migrating peoples entered the British Isles. These were, for example, the peoples belonging to the Bell Beaker culture, which existed from roughly 2,800 to 2,300 BC in Europe but lasted in Britain until 1,800 BC. Bell Beaker peoples were likely migrants, spreading their culture through both trade and migratory routes. We must remember that trade connections were not uncommon in this period of history. In fact, it was a major way to spread new trends, technologies, and influence other peoples. In time, the Bell Beaker traditions brought the classic Bronze Age traditions into the British Isles, Scotland included.

By the late Bronze Age period, this culture was replaced by the one newly arriving from mainland Europe: the Urnfield Culture. It was called thus because of its unique tradition of cremating the dead and placing the ashes in urns and burying these in the fields. The culture likely spread into the British Isles through trade and influence, and it began roughly around 1,200 BC. Scholars believe that it is during this time that the Proto-Celtic languages reached the British Isles and took hold there. For years there was an ongoing debate: whether the Celtic-speaking peoples invaded the region, or the language was simply adopted. Modern research suggests that the case is of the latter: it is much more plausible that no sort of warfare was involved. In fact, it is much more probable that these Celtic languages were a sort of "lingua franca", a commonly used language in Europe that was used in trading, politics, and so on, much like the English language is today. In time, with frequent use and a far reach, the proto-Celtic language became the dominant one in the British Isles. But not just the language - the proto-Celtic traditions and cultural traits also took root.

In mainland Europe, the Urnfield Culture was followed by the Hallstatt Culture. The latter one is commonly associated with the Celtic populations that we know in history. Through trading, cultural diffusion, and limited migrations, this culture reached Britain and Ireland as well. Either way, our knowledge of the very ancient inhabitants of Scotland are limited at best. The path from the early Bronze Age inhabitants that created the Knap of Howar, Skara Brae, or the many standing stone circles across Scotland and in the Orkneys; to the peoples that lived in the very early Iron Age, a few thousands of years later - is, at best, murky. But what little we know of the ancient inhabitants of Scotland tells us that the ages of cultural diffusion and movements of people, as well as trading contacts, all worked their way towards the emergence of a unique people: fierce highlanders and island-dwellers, proud of their Scottish identity and protective of their home.

By the time the Romans took interest in the British Isles, however, first written mention of Scotland's inhabitants began to appear. By far the most well-known were the Picts. Still, the subject of the Picts is for the most part frustrating - historians simply don't know all that much about them, particularly because of a significant lack of written records and archaeological material. Nevertheless, scholars agree that the Picts were likely a confederation of Iron Age tribes that formed in the central and eastern parts of Scotland, likely speaking a version of an insular Celtic language which was closely related to the Brittonic , spoken by Britons to the South. Interestingly, several early Medieval history accounts, such as the writings of ancient historiographers Bede, Holinshed, or Geoffrey of Monmouth, as well as the monumental works like the Pictish Chronicle and the Anglo-Saxon Chronicle all mention the Picts to be the "conquerors of Alba from Scythia". Alas, no substantial evidence exists to prove that ancient claim. Furthermore, it is believed that the name Picts was given to them by the ancient Romans, and that the name stems from the word "pictus" meaning "painted". This name was possibly given to them because of their tradition of tattooing that was practiced amongst many peoples in the ancient times. However, there are other likely explanations, such as the relation to a Gallic tribe from southern France, called the Pictones. Either way, the identity, name, and origins of the Picts remain a subject of much debate today: history simply doesn't preserve them all that well. What is more, there are some indications that the Picts had an altogether different name for themselves: Albidosi. This is a name mentioned in the short Chronicle of the Kings of Alba.

To better understand the ethnogenesis of the Scottish people, we must also touch upon the history of the Hebrides, the west of Scotland, and the famed Dal Riata. Dal Riata was a Gaelic kingdom, existing from roughly the 5th century AD, extending on both sides of the North Channel. It consisted of small parts of northeastern Ireland - namely the northern part of the modern County Antrim in Ireland - and much of the Inner Hebrides of Scotland, as well as parts of Argyll. Before this point, Irish Gaels emigrated in large numbers across the channel, settling in Scotland (Pictish lands), namely in the Hebridean islands. The history of the kingdom of Dal Riata was marked by early ups - and many later "downs". In Ireland, the kingdom lost all influence and power following the Viking invasions of the 9th century, while the Scottish part of the kingdom was kept "in check" by the constant wars with the Picts. But this part of history is important for another reason - the emergence of the Scots. The name Scoti (Scotti) was a Latin name first documented in the 3rd century AD. Initially, it was the name Romans attributed to the Gaels in the British Isles. But over time, it became reserved exclusively for the Gaels living in the area of Scotland. The exact meaning of the name Scoti remains unclear, with numerous theories pushed forward, but without any substantial evidence for an exact meaning. Either way, the unique identity that formed from the migrations of Irish Gaels into the west of the Pictish lands, was the key aspect of the formation of the modern Scottish identity. In time, the land of the Scoti became known as Scotia, and later as Scotland.

Although the Gaelic kingdom of Dal Riata was devastated and conquered by the King of the Picts, Angus son of Fergus, in the mid 700's, the language and the cultural traits of the Gaels remained. In time, the whole of the north of Britain was known as Scotland. The Brythonic Celtic language of the Picts was gradually replaced by a Goidelic language, known as Scots Gaelic. This language - together with the Irish and Manx - developed from the Old Irish. After all, time and influence work together, and can be detrimental to the identity of a sovereign nation. The once-proud land of the Picts simply could not survive the movements of the ages, and the pressures and influences from the invading neighboring cultures. The Anglo-Saxons invading Britain in the South contributed to the extinction of the Brittonic language, to which Pictish was related. And together with the emergence of the Gaelic-speaking Dal Riata, the Pictish language simply stood no chance of persevering through the centuries. And, as we all know, language is the foundation of national identity: once it is lost and forgotten, so is the nation that once used it. By 1100 AD, the Pictish language was fully extinct. The Picts were likewise fully "gaelicized" by that time, and became known as Scots, with the Pictish identity fully forgotten. However, in many ways, history dictated the fates of many ethnicities in the British Isles. The amalgamation of the Irish Gaels and the Picts resulted in the emergence of the Kingdom of Alba - or the Kingdom of Scotland, which lay the foundations for the emergence of the modern nation of Scotland.

By 43 AD, the Romans at last descended upon the Celtic-speaking tribes of Britain. The conquest undoubtedly destabilized the region and affected these peoples in a major way. But even before the conquest began, the early Roman navigators and explorers tried to gain more knowledge of these distant and hitherto unknown islands in the North Atlantic. The earliest accounts come from a famed Greek explorer, Pytheas of Massalia. He is said to have circumnavigated the British Isles sometime around 325 BC, during his explorations of northwestern Europe. His original writings of his travels did not survive in their original form, but his work was later cited by other classical authors. Either way, Pytheas was the first to give us names we know even today: he mentions the islands of Ierne and Albion (Ireland and Britain respectively), as well as the most northerly point of the isles - the *Orcas* (Orkney). It is undoubted that all these names Pytheas learned from the native inhabitants, and that they are all Celtic in origin.

By the time of the legendary Pliny the Elder, around the time of the Roman invasion of Britain, the knowledge of the British Isles was expanded considerably. The Romans thus knew of the Hebudes (the Hebrides), Dumna (likely the Outer Hebrides, named after the tribe of Dumnonii), as well as the Caledonian Forest. Furthermore, they could name a number of tribes dwelling in both Britain and Scotland, the chief of these being the Picts as we said, as well as Caledonii. However, the accounts of Pliny the Elder tell us that the Roman knowledge of interior Scotland was highly limited, and that all that they knew was ascertained from the sea and the coastlines. Entering Scotland was a big challenge for the Romans. Nevertheless, in true Roman spirit, they did try to fully invade the North of Britain too. When the Brythonic tribes were subdued, and the Roman province of Britannia created, the Roman commanders could shift their attention to the north - towards modern Scotland. The invasion of this region began around 71 AD, led by the governor Quintus Petillius Cerialis. However, he was soon replaced by a much more able and far better known general - Gnaeus Julius Agricola. This new commander arrived in Britain in AD 78, and soon after began a series of major incursions into Scotland.

These early operations were marked by a number of successes, although detailed information is lacking. The Romans were able to penetrate "to the estuary of River Taus", which was likely the Roman name for River Tay. And wherever the Romans gained a foothold, they built forts and camps to keep a hold of their territorial gains. So it was that Agricola created the legionary fortress at Inchtuthil, which existed for some 7 years in total. Interestingly, archeologists discovered a curious Roman hoard at Inchtuthil, which consisted of some 900,000 iron nails of various sizes! One theory states that these nails were buried by the fleeing Romans so that the native tribes could not use them for their own gains.

Roman accounts then mention a series of deeper penetrations by Agricola, and a famed battle of Mons Graupius, fought in AD 84. The authenticity of this battle was never fully ascertained by historians, nor its exact location. Roman accounts were also considered as biased when describing the battle, which was claimed as a decisive and total Roman victory. The fact that the accounts cite Roman casualties as just 380 auxiliaries in comparison to 10,000 Caledonian tribesmen on the opposing side led historians to doubt the battle's credibility. Nevertheless, we know for a fact that following this year, the Romans established a series of forts along the so-called "Gask Ridge", a line which effectively established a boundary between the Highlands and the Lowlands. This was thus known as the first "limes" - a Roman frontier line - in Scotland. However, the Romans were never fully invested into the conquest of Scotland.

The commanders that came after Agricola were either unable - or unwilling - to continue further conquest of Scotland. Due to this, the Roman frontier line kept receding gradually. First the line was pushed back between the Solway Firth and the Tyne, and in the end, the Roman forces withdrew altogether to a line in what is now Northern England. This line was the famous Hadrian's Wall, an immense fortification that ran from coast to coast. It is the largest Roman archeological feature in the whole of Britain, and it has a length of 73 miles (117.5 kilometers). The wall was there to mark the boundary between the Roman province of Brittania and the unconquered "Caledonia" - or Scotland. Some scholars propose that the wall was there to prevent the powerful tribe of the Brigantes (dwelling in Britain) to unite with the Scottish tribes such as the Caledonii.

Soon after the Hadrian's Wall was made, the Romans decided to push deeper into Scotland once again. This allowed them to construct a new frontier, deeper inland, which was known as the Antonine Wall, finished around 154 AD. But once again, the Romans realized that the

Scottish tribes could not be subdued: after just a few years of being manned, the wall was overrun and abandoned, with the Romans once again retreating further back to the Hadrian's Wall.

The Turmoil in the British Isles: Angles, Saxons, and the Norse

As we all know, however, the Roman era was slowly coming to a halt. The great crisis of their realm was ongoing in central Europe, and that crisis was bound to reflect on their rule in the British Isles. Following their retreat to Hadrian's Wall, the Romans never really attempted to conquer or enter Scotland ever again. The wall acted as a Roman frontier - until that frontier collapsed in the 5th century, together with the Roman rule in Britain. Due to all this, the Roman influence - such as their language, customs, and traditions - never fully took hold in Scotland, allowing the fierce tribes to continue their own culture undisturbed. The Picts remained a dominant entity in the northern parts of Scotland, with the other tribes occupying the other regions.

History then rolled on with the events that were very much centered on southern Britain, i.e., England. With the gradual retreat of the Romans, this region was left as a vulnerable realm ripe for the taking. The Germanic invaders - the Angles, Saxons, and the Jutes - seized this chance and began a gradual conquest of Britain. Still, the Anglo-Saxon conquest of this land would not touch upon Scotland - initially. In fact, Scotland was left with its own petty kingdoms and realms which often warred with one another. In the North there were the Picts, with their petty kingdoms of Fortriu and Alba, in the west the Gaelic-speaking Scots of the Dal Riata, and in the south was a Brythonic kingdom of Strathclyde. The Anglo-Saxons did not wage war within these lands directly, however, they brought with them Christianity and a wholly new era of the early Medieval ages. This brought changes in Britain and Ireland - changes that were bound to influence Scotland sooner or later. Thus began the gradual Christianization of the Picts, mostly through the Scots-Irish missionaries, such as Saint Columba. The Scots of the Dal Riata maintained strong links with Ireland, and Christianity quickly spread through Scotland through the Hebrides. Scholars believe that it was exactly Christianity and missionary work that contributed to the gradual disappearance of the Picts - or their increased "Gaelicization". With the Scots (Gael) religion, they also adopted their language and customs, generation by generation. In time, the Pictish identity and language were getting forgotten. And with the merger of the crowns of Dal Riata and the Picts, and the rise of the Kingdom Of Alba, the Picts were bound to be forgotten, and a new realm began to emerge: Scotland.

Greatly contributing to the gradual disappearance of the Picts, as well as contributing to the identity of the Scots overall, were also the raids of the Vikings. These ferocious Norsemen, sailing out from their ports in Denmark, Sweden, and Norway, came into the European public view with a catastrophic surprise. Sailing across the North Sea, they raided the English monastery at Lindisfarne in 793 AD, shocking the world as they did so. This event ushered Europe into the Viking Age, which was to last from 793 AD until 1066 AD. The Vikings were highly successful seafarers, relying on diplomacy, trade, and straight-out plunder to make their achievements possible. For the land of Scotland, the appearance of the Norsemen had many consequences. The de-stabilization which these invasions caused was a likely contributor to the rapid Gaelicization of the Picts. In Scotland, the outlying islands, such as the Inner and Outer Hebrides, the Orkneys and the Shetland islands, directly in the path of the seafaring Vikings, became a point of much contention between various ruling powers. But above all, the presence of the Vikings in these islands left great marks on their emerging identity, placenames, and cultural traits. Much of the names in the Orkneys, Shetland, and Hebrides are Norse. Still, all this just contributed to the unique fighting spirit of the Scottish people, and their ferocious North Atlantic identity. In the core of the Scottish lands, Viking presence was - for the most part - not seen. It was reserved only for the "ocean-facing" areas - the shores and islands. However, the great political calamity that the Vikings caused in the British Isles, certainly left a mark on the emerging Scottish Kingdom. After all, who knows? If it weren't for the Vikings and their destructive raids, Scotland would have perhaps never gotten a chance at fighting for its independence.

Did You Know?

The Gallowglass were a class of elite mercenary warriors of Norse-Gaelic origins, hailing from Western Scotland, primarily the Hebrides. Known as "gallóglaigh" (foreign warriors), and "gall gaeil" (foreign Gaels), they were feared across Europe, and highly sought after as mercenaries. A principal fighting force in the British Isles in Medieval times, their origins lie with the Vikings who settled in the Scottish isles and mixed with the native Gaels. This Norse-Gaelic culture was known for its ferocity and power: one source from 1600 describes these warriors as "cruel without compassion, men of great and mighty bodies, who would rather die than yield". And truly, many records mention that Gallowglass mercenaries simply did not yield in the face of overwhelming odds: many are the cases where they simply fought until death. However, their ferocity in battle held quite a reputation. A band of gallowglasses being present at a battlefield could often be enough to shake the enemy's morale and turn the tide of the battle.

The Early Origins of Scotland: Kingdom of Alba

In many ways, it was Christianity that laid the foundation of what is now modern Scotland. If not, then it certainly gave the Scottish rulers a "nudge in the right direction", pushing it in line with the other fast-developing realms of the Early Middle Ages. Around this time, while the threat of the Vikings dominated politics in the Anglo-Saxon realm, a new ruler in Scotland appeared. This was the famed Cínaed mac Ailpín (Kenneth MacAlpin), known as Kenneth I. He inherited the throne of Dal Riata from his father, and began a stellar rise to power, conquering the Kingdom of the Picts between 843 and 850 AD. This man is traditionally considered the founder of Scotland, being perhaps the first king of Alba. In the meantime, the realm of the Anglo-Saxons suffered heavily at the hands of the Vikings, who managed to seize the south of Northumbria around 867 and create the Kingdom of York. This undoubtedly affected the development of early Scotland. But the true early rise of medieval Scotland began with one of the first successors of Kenneth MacAlpin - his great-great-great-grandson, Constantine II. Known in Gaelic as Causantin Mac Aeda, this ruler was born no later than 879 AD, and died around 952 AD. Around his time, the name Kingdom of Alba - used to denote Scotland - first began to appear and be actively used - both in Scotland, and outside of it. Constantine, and the rulers that came before him, first began to respond to the overwhelming threat of the Vikings. The kingdom's capital had to be relocated in these decades, due to the encroachment of these north men from the coasts inland. The reign of Constantine II was one of the longest in the history of Scotland, surpassed only by King William the Lion in the early 1600's. His lengthy - and for the most part successful - reign is seen by historians as the crucial part of Scotland's formative period. During his reign, the Kingdom of Alba fought with numerous enemies, chiefly with the Northmen, the Anglo-Saxons, and the Welsh of Cumberland. However, sides were changed towards the end of Constantine's reign. When he was forced to face the ambitious Anglo-Saxon ruler, Aethelstan, Constantine sided with the Viking King of Dublin, Olaf III Guthfrithson and with the King of Strathclyde, Owain ap Dyfnwal. Together, they marched to face Aethelstan, having realized in previous years that this powerful English ruler could only be defeated by an alliance of his enemies. These forces clashed in the monumental Battle of Brunanburh, around 937 AD. However, Olaf, Constantine, and Owain were decisively defeated by the Anglo-Saxons, and their army devastated and routed. Ancient writers mention this clash as:

"A great battle, lamentable and terrible was cruelly fought... in which fell uncounted thousands of the Northmen... And on the other side, a multitude of Saxons fell; but Athelstan, the King of the Saxons, obtained a great victory."

Some sources incorrectly state that Constantine fell dead in this battle. Truth is, he did not. In fact, his reign continued until roughly 943 AD, when he abdicated and retreated to a monastery. The Battle of Brunanburh was one of the defining events of this period. It was one of the first in the string of many conflicts between England and Scotland, and it also marked the point of beginning of English nationalism. With his decisive victory, Aethelstan prevented the dissolution of England, but he could not, alas, unite the whole island into one realm: Strathclyde and Scotland both remained independent for the time being. Furthermore, many scholars agree that Brunanburh was the "single most important Anglo-Saxon battle before Hastings in 1066".

"The Danes of Northumbria and Norfolk entered into a confederacy [against Æthelstan], which was joined by Constantine, king of the Scots, and many others; on which [Æthelstan] levied an army and led it into

Northumbria. On his way, he was met by many pilgrims returning homeward from Beverley... [Æthelstan] offered his poniard upon the holy altar [at Beverley], and made a promise that, if the lord would grant him victory over his enemies, he would redeem the said poniard at a suitable price, which he accordingly did.... In the battle which was fought on this occasion there fell Constantine, king of Scots, and five other kings, twelve earls, and an infinite number of the lower classes, on the side of the barbarians."

Nevertheless, no matter how brutal and devastating this battle was, it still secured a deal of peace and prosperity for the whole of Britain. Many historians state that the battle was extremely bloody, and - at the day's end - indecisive. It is due to this indecisiveness (Aethelstan still claimed victory), that the English could not pursue and conquer parts of Alba. To that end, the island remained divided between the Celtic North, and the Anglo-Saxon South.

Strathclyde's power waned in these years, and the Scottish ruler Mael Coluim I (Malcolm I), managed to annex Strathclyde as part of a deal with the English King Edmund. This fact shows us that Scotland had great authority in the region of Strathclyde in the late stages of the 9th century. And this was just the first in a generational series of expansions that saw Scotland rising to a formidable state with boundaries much alike those of today. Around 1018, the Northumbrian forces were defeated by the Scottish ruler Malcolm II, at the crucial Battle of Carham. The Scots faced the Northumbrians, who were led by Uhtred the Bold of Bamburgh, and decisively routed them. This victory allowed the Scots to expand further, establishing their eastern boundary at the River Tweed. Lothian was thence a part of Scotland. Around the same time, Malcolm's grandson, Duncan, became the King of Strathclyde. This meant that once he succeeded his grandfather at the Scottish throne, the boundaries of the Kingdom were greatly expanded. And from all this, we can see that with just three generations of successful Scottish Kings, the nation grew immensely in power. The success began with Constantine II (reigned 900 to 943), continued with Kenneth II (r. 971 to 995), and culminated with Malcolm II (1005 to 1034).

In time, the Viking (Norwegian) grip on Scotland's lands loosened. The Viking Age was coming to a rapid end, and the Norwegian attempts to remain a formidable force in the British Isles were finally crushed with their devastating defeat at the hands of the Anglo-Saxons at the Battle of Stamford Bridge in 1066. The Scots, however, still had to deal with them, as the Hebridean islands became a part of Scotland only in 1266, while the Orkneys and Shetland were under Norwegian rule until the 15th century.

In 1066, the British Isles were once again shaken, but this time by a calamity much greater than the Vikings. Because in this year, attempting to exploit the succession crisis in England, the Norman Duke William the Bastard sailed across the English channel with a massive army and utterly defeated the Anglo-Saxons at the iconic Battle of Hastings. The defeat of the English marked an entirely new chapter in the history of the British Isles. The Normans brought with them a new language and the concept of European feudalism and extensive castle building. England was soon fully dominated by these rulers, and Ireland would soon follow as well. And the invasion would certainly reflect on Scotland, too. Namely, things for Scotland would change with the rise of a new young ruler - Máel Coluim III, better known as Malcolm Canmore. Around 1040, one of the Mormaers of Moray - which was a semi-independent region in Scotland - named Mac Bethad (MacBeth), rose to power and killed the King of Scotland, Duncan. He then ruled as King for seventeen years. Malcolm Canmore was the son and heir of Duncan and had no intention of abandoning his rightful throne. He fled to the court of Edward the Confessor, the English King, biding his time. In 1057, with the aid of the Saxon forces, he returned to Scotland and ousted MacBeth, killing him and becoming the rightful King of Scotland. Malcolm's reign was good, but he would be remembered for different things entirely. First was his marriage to an English princess, Margaret (later a saint of the Catholic Church), and the second was a series of unsuccessful attempts to Conquer the English region of Northumbria and further expand the Scottish realm.

Malcolm's ambitions would prove costly: the Norman ruler, William the Conqueror, responded in kind, penetrating deep into Scotland and forcing Malcolm Canmore to finally swear fealty to him. This opened Scotland to later claims of sovereignty by the Kings of England - claims that would greatly dictate and disturb Scottish independence and prosperity. And with the Normans, new changes appeared in Scottish society. At first, William the Conqueror was content with allowing the line of Canmore to reign as it did: he kept Scotland "in line" with sheer military pressure. But the Scottish nobles and the ruling family could not ignore the success and the prosperity of the Normans in England, brought entirely through their feudal system. So, in no time, this iconic medieval system found its way into Scotland, which was at the time still a clan-based society. The Scottish ruling family began inviting Norman nobles into Scotland, to rule over estates, and these nobles introduced the successful (but oppressive) feudal system. Many modern Scottish clans can trace their origins to Norman nobles. For example, the most powerful of these early Norman noble houses were the *Comyns* - known in Scotland as the Cummings.

But it wasn't just the feudal system that came with the Normans. It was also a new language. In the Lowlands region, a distinct form of English began to be actively used, instigated by the new nobility, as well as by the church. Thus, actively emerging, was the Scots language, a sister language of the English, although quite different from it, infused with Scottish accents, dialectisms, and Gaelic loanwords.

So, as we can see, the arrival of the Normans did not only change England from roots up, but it also began changing Scotland, too. In the views of many, this was generally undermining the progress of an independent, fledgling Alba. Just as it began to rise on its own, with its unique Gaelic identity, the Normans arrived and plunged it again into centuries of foreign influence and mainland European rules and traditions. Still, the majority of these cultural, linguistic, and judicial changes were reserved for the ruling class - the Kings and the clergy. The common folk, those hardy highland shepherds and warriors, the clansmen and the merchants, they still retained their distinct "Picto-Gaelic" identity and language. The Gaelic language, one of the cornerstones of Scottish identity, remained actively used - mostly in the Highlands. In the Lowlands, the English-influenced Scots language was predominant.

The full force of the Norman influence began to be seen in Scotland by the time of King David I - Dauíd mac Maíl Choluim. This was the youngest son of Malcolm Canmore, and he became King from 1124 AD. However, to take the Scottish throne, he had to engage in 10 years of civil war against his own nephew, Máel Coluim mac Alaxandair. The rise of David brought a series of immense changes into Scotland - changes which were begun during the reign of Malcolm Canmore. This period is known in history as the "Davidian Revolution". David began an almost forced introduction of English laws, customs, and institutions into Scotland. It has been agreed that his policies greatly undermined the development of independent Scotland in the later Medieval period.

Scotland's Earliest Kings: From Malcolm to David, and Onwards

Of course, David I knew quite well what potential the English (Norman) style of ruling had. Before becoming king, he spent most of his life as an Earl of (English) Lothian, and resided mostly at the court of King Henry I, the English King who was also his brother-in-law. In England, he was essentially a Norman French baron, and became closely associated with the most prominent Norman nobles, such as William de Somerville, Earl Gospatric, Bernard I de Balliol, and others. And so, once he came to the Scottish throne, David was more Norman English than he was Scottish: introducing these radical changes into Scotland was his first and foremost task. He granted all of these Norman nobles charters of land all across Scotland, making them prominent nobles and introducing feudal rule across the nation. Robert de Bruce gained Annandale, Renfrew and North Kyle went to Walter FitzAlan, Ranulf de Sules gained Liddesdale, Hugh de Morville acquired Lauderdale and Cunningham, while Eskdale went to Robert Avenel. Amongst these Normans was the cadet branch of the famed FitzAlan Norman house. They would later become known as the Stewarts and then as Stuarts, becoming the royal family of Great Britain.

Of course, these pro-English changes introduced by David I were not uncontested by the native Scottish nobility. The early years of David's rule were marked with great discontent and internal warfare. The conflicts were headed by the Celtic claimants to the throne, the MacHeths. These powerful Earls of Moray led by Earl Angus, were finally defeated by David's forces in 1130 AD, close to North Esk in Forfarshire. The final defeat of the Scottish opposition gave David a chance to once and for all extinguish the ancient Gaelic Earldom of Moray, which was for centuries the home of native Gaelic pretenders to the throne of Scotland. Following this, David continued his policies of anglicization of Scotland. The Normans introduced the practice of increased castle building, and feudal land tenure. The court became Anglo-Norman in style, and the system of burghs and market towns was established. There was now a greater authoritative control over the country, especially in the Lowlands, with the introduction of a royal Justiciar, and regional Sheriffs. Of course, this was not all entirely grim per se: the establishment of royal Burghs and the granting of charters led to the development of first true cities in Scotland and helped boost the nation's economy substantially.

Without a doubt, the policies of David I served to further divide Scotland into an English-influenced south, and the traditional Gaelic North-west. For generations after, the true strength of the Gaelic Scots was centered in the western regions of Lochaber, Kintyre, Moidart, Knoydart, Morar and Mamore, as well as in the Hebridean islands. And the Feudal power following David's rule only expanded further, reaching Angus, Perth, Aberdeen, Moray, and Strathclyde.

David's rule was also marked by his endless pretensions to the English Earldom of Northumberland, an undoubtedly lucrative prize that would greatly expand his Scottish Kingdom. Around 1135, with the death of the English King Henry I, David set about claiming what he desired. His own niece, Matilda, was embroiled in a power struggle for the English throne. David backed her, opposing Stephen of Bloise, and crossed into England with a sizable army. However, he was not successful. His son Henry, another pretender, only received Carlisle and Huntingdon, with his claim to Northumberland largely ignored. But David was not dismayed. In 1138 he tried again, this time with an enormous army from the entire Scotland. He entered England and clashed with the English army on August 22nd, 1138, at the Battle of Cowton Moor (Battle of the Standard). This was a decisive engagement in David's struggle for Northumberland. Initially, he had an upper hand against the English, managing to devastate their heavily armored troops. But in a turn of events, possibly due to the overextension of his lines, David's Scottish troops broke and fled when a false rumor of David's death was spread amongst the men. Retreating, David was forced to fight a series of defensive rearguard actions on his way back to Carlisle, suffering heavy losses along the way. The English claimed victory, although barely.

"But of David's army nearly ten thousand fell in different places, and as many as fifty were captured of his picked men. But the king's son came on foot with one knight only to Carlisle, while his father scarce escaped through woods and passes to Roxburgh. Of two hundred mailed knights whom [David] had, only nineteen brought back their hauberks, because each had abandoned as booty to the foe almost everything that he had. And thus, very great spoils were taken from his army, as well of horses and arms and raiment as of very many other things."

Yet even with this loss, David I gained his ultimate goal - Northumberland. His own son, Henry, gained - through peaceful arrangements - the Earldom of Northumberland, albeit devoid of two crucial strongholds, Bamborough and Newcastle. However, the successes were not destined to last. King David suffered an immense blow in 1152, when his only son and heir, Henry, unexpectedly died - likely from an illness. David died one year later, in 1153, but not before appointing his grandson, Malcolm IV as his heir. And although the eldest of Henry's sons, Malcolm IV was just 10 years old at the time. Still, he was King of Scotland from 1153 until 1165, when he died, ill and unmarried at age 24. He was succeeded by his younger brother William, known as "the Lion", who ruled for an incredible 49 years - the second longest reign in the history of Scotland.

How was the new feudal system, introduced by David, reflected in Medieval Scotland? Let us not forget that the large parts of the

Highlands were still in many ways rooted in archaic ways of life, remote and wild. There is no doubt that the arrival of the then "modern" customs of Norman rule were hard to apply to the Highland way of life. However, there were no exceptions. The Scottish crown wanted to incorporate every corner of the realm - no matter how remote or Gaelic it was - under its new pro-European feudal system. Still, some of the traditional Scottish traditions were similar to certain feudal traits, and the two could match to an extent. The unwritten Celtic law dictated, in theory, that the tribe or clan as a whole, was the source of property in land. Families could hold lands in tenure, and later turn it into permanent property if they could acquire an abundance of oxen, i.e., wealth. It is important to remember that across the Gaelic world, the oxen were the real true wealth and power. The more oxen a chief had, the more powerful he was. This led to the tradition of cattle raiding amongst feuding clans. This practice is firmly rooted in Gaelic cultures, predominantly in Ireland and Scotland. Special "Watches" evolved in the highland, protecting cattle herds in exchange for money. It was in essence an extortion racket.

The Feudal system of the Middle Ages revolved around the "protection" of the villagers by a feudal lord or knight, in exchange for service and taxation. In Scotland, specifically in the Highlands, where actual money was somewhat scarcely used, the poor clansmen had to pay their rents and taxes in physical labor and various services to a lord. Taxation was often done in physical goods, such as food, animals, or even manure. But there was something that every clansman had, no matter their financial status, that the lords valued greatly - their physical strength. By far the most valuable thing that a tenant could provide for his lord was, of course, military service. Though dwelling in the remotest parts of Scotland, and no matter how poor and destitute, a clansman could still hold a spear and a sword. And thus, when a noble lord "called his banners", i.e., assembled an army, the tenants under his rule had to obey and provide military service. But below even the poorest of clansmen, there were those poorer still. These were the "unfree" serfs, who enjoyed no freedoms and no privileges. They worked the lands for their lord and were generally a part of the land itself - they were freely handed over as a form of currency. However, the Church worked intensely on rooting out the practice of serfdom and was even backed by some of the lords - since a serf, once freed, was useful as a soldier.

Nevertheless, it was noted that the new feudal practices penetrated somewhat slowly into the remote Scottish parts, notably in the West Highlands and across the Hebridean Isles. These lands were rugged, wild, and mountainous, and almost devoid of towns, and thus, the written laws of the Lowland Scottish court were slower to reach them.

Did You Know?

The Scottish Clan is one of the foremost aspects of the Scottish identity. Scotland has around 500 separate clans, both those with chiefs, and those without one. Throughout the centuries, the Scottish clan was an invaluable aspect of the Scottish social system. It is a kindred, a social group that is often connected to a specific place of origin within Scotland, and to a certain lineage. Many clans can track their origins to hazy ancient times, to Gaelic chiefs and Pictish Kings. Others, on the other hand, originate in the Middle Ages, and the arrival of powerful Norman lords. A clan name belongs to the chief and his lineage but was often adopted by subjects and tenants under his protection. Some of the most prominent Scottish clans are MacDonald, MacGregor, Fraser, Armstrong, Blackadder, Bruce, Hamilton, MacLeod, Gordon, Buchanan, MacDougall, MacQuarrie, MacAlister, and many, many others, each with its own intriguing history.

The long reign of William the Lion, David's grandson, was marked with further progress of Medieval Scotland, and many new achievements.

William continued improving and building upon his grandfather's policies and innovations, solidifying Scotland's path towards success and independence as a sovereign nation. In contrast with his predecessor, Malcolm IV, who was frail, religious, and died young, William the Lion was for the most part a confident, headstrong, and decisive King. Note that he was not called "the Lion" during his lifetime: the nickname came later in history and is connected with his royal banner that displayed a lion rampant. However, although an efficient monarch, William's reign saw increased hostilities with England.

Early on after coming to the throne, William attempted to regain control of Northumbria, which was once more subjected to the rule of the Anglo-Norman crown. Initially, he was present at the royal court of the English King Henry II, but soon enough the two monarchs quarreled. As a direct consequence of this, William the Lion was responsible for creating the first definite alliance treaty between Scotland and France, in 1168 AD, strengthening his position within European geopolitics. Around this time, a rebellion broke out in England, directed against the unpopular King Henry II Curtmantle (Henry FitzEmpress). Three of the king's sons, his French wife, Eleanor of Aquitaine, and their various supporters led a revolt from April 1173 until September 1174 AD. William the Lion was also involved in the rebellion, siding with the rebels against the English King. However, he did not present himself admirably in this event: in 1174, during one of his raids into Northumberland, William got himself captured rather foolishly. This occurred during the Battle of Alnwick: he allowed himself to be taken by surprise, with his army scattered and spread out. After a brief melee, William was captured alive and taken in fetters to Newcastle. From there, he was transported to Falaise in Normandy, while the English King occupied great parts of Scotland. Afterwards, Henry Curthose offered him a chance to buy his freedom and to regain his kingdom - although at a heavy price. Firstly, William had to recognize the English King as his feudal superior, to subject the Scottish Church to that of England, and to pay for the cost of the English occupation of Scotland. This meant that the key Scottish castles would be garrisoned by English men, and the Scottish King had to pay for it. William, of course, had to agree to these humiliating terms: he signed the Treaty of Falaise in December 1174, and eventually officially swore fealty to King Henry II at York in 1175. For the next 15 years, William the Lion was subjected to rather humiliating English overlordship: he had to seek English permission for virtually any important decision, and the humiliation went as far as Henry II choosing William's bride.

Of course, the humiliation of English occupation caused internal troubles as well: a revolt broke out in Scotland, in Galloway, and raged on until 1186. At the time, William had to consider the potential threat of the Norse Earls of Orkney (Orkney was still Norwegian at the time) and wanted to prevent them benefiting from the situation by invading mainland Scotland. To that end, William's reign was marked with increased castle building towards the northern shores. The instability continued, however, with the additional revolt in 1181, started by Donald MacWilliams, a descendant of the Scottish King Duncan II. The struggle involved Inverness, which William the Lion could only retake after Donald MacWilliams died in 1187. Only by 1202 was this domestic threat finally settled.

A Lasting Feud: The Conflicts With the English

Still, even with all these events unfolding, Scotland saw a period of moderate prosperity during William's long reign. After some brief quarrels with Pope Alexander III, William managed to succeed in gaining a quite important papal bull in 1188 - which declared that the Church of Scotland was subject directly to none other than Rome. In the following year, the humiliating effects of the Treaty of Falaise were at last terminated, this time by the new English King, Richard the Lionheart. By December 5th, 1189, the treaty was no more, and that allowed William to again focus on his internal affairs - free from English interference. Almost at once, he set about "reconquering" the parts of his Kingdom that were affected by revolt and insurrection. He reasserted his authority in Galloway, conducted a number of campaigns that brought Sutherland and Caithness back under his command, and finally quelled the revolts in Moray and Inverness. With this, the authority of the Crown of Scotland was finally spread across Scotland as we know it today.

By the early 1200's, however, William the Lion was aging and frail, and the tensions with England did not cease - even though Scotland was once again independent. In order to exploit William's apparent weakness, the English - now led by King John - antagonized the Scots by marching a huge army close to Berwick. William was forced to resolve the situation by offering money, as well as his daughters' hands in marriage to English nobles. Furthermore, his heir, Alexander, had to marry John's eldest daughter, Joan. With that marriage, the English court once more held pretensions to the crown of Scotland.

Yet, when all is said and done, William the Lion's reign was marked with steady progress and many achievements. The successes (although pro-Norman and progressive) of David I, were not forsaken, and his successor steadily built upon them. William brought into Scotland new prosperous burghs, extended feudalization, a great increase of trade, solid and clarified criminal law, and increased responsibilities of sheriffs and justiciars - all of which brought law and stability into Scotland. Upon his death, he was an admired and respected monarch. He was succeeded by his only surviving son and heir, Alexander II - Alasdair Mac Uilleim.

The reign of young Alexander began in many ways just like his father's: just one year after coming to the throne, in 1215, he had to deal with two Scottish clans that at once turned to revolt - the MacHeths and the MacWilliams. The latter clan was that of the descendants of one of the grandsons of Malcolm Canmore, the King of Scots. They raised a number of rebellions in an attempt to claim the Scottish throne for themselves. However, Alexander quickly reacted to their insurrection, putting a quick end to it. Almost immediately afterwards, he was involved in a rebellion against the English King John - supporting the cause of the rebellious English barons. In response to the Scottish threat, King John ravaged the north, chiefly the prosperous burgh of Berwick. However, in a complicated turn of events, with King John dying in the meantime, the new English King, a boy of nine years, Henry III, was accepted by the rebelled barons, leading to peace - and the signing of the Treaty of Kingston. The tensions were thus calmed, and the Scottish and English crown reconciled with the marriage of Alexander and the young English princess Joan.

But what of the Norwegians, you might ask yourself? How was Scotland of the mid 1200s affected by the aging threat of those fierce Northerners? The truth is, by 1200s time, the Viking age was already at its last legs. The Norwegians held the Orkneys and the Shetland isles, and parts of Caithness too - as part of the Jarldom of Orkney. In 1222, Alexander exerted his authority across the whole of Caithness, following an incident in which the Jarl of Orkney was implicated in a heinous crime of burning a Christian Bishop alive in his hall. Furthermore, he managed to put parts of Argyll under his command as well. But the Norwegians will come into play towards the end of Alexander's reign - and we'll mention them soon enough. First, we will mention another significant event related to the rule of Alexander II. This was the important Treaty of York, signed in 1237 with the English King, which clearly defined the boundaries between England and Scotland - boundaries that are largely unchanged today.

Towards the end of his reign, Alexander sought to expand his kingdom to include the traditionally Scottish Western Isles. A part of the Hebrides, these islands were under Norwegian rule, known to them as the "Southern Isles". Initially, he sought to acquire them peacefully, by negotiations and offers to purchase them - but the Norwegians declined him repeatedly. This then turned into a dispute, and Alexander set about conquering the islands by force. However, he died en-route, in 1249, after catching a fever on the isle of Kerrera in the Inner Hebrides. The dispute over the Hebrides with the Norwegians wouldn't be resolved until 1266 AD, when the Norwegian King at last ceded them to Scotland, alongside Isle of Man. Today, we can only wonder what the outcome would be of Alexander's attempt to wrest the Hebrides out of Norwegian hands. A new war? A successful expansion of the Scottish kingdom? Many things could have been different if fever did not claim Alexander's life. Either way, his reign ended abruptly, and he was succeeded by his only son and heir, Alexander III - a boy of seven. It took young Alexander III thirteen years to continue the disputes over the Hebrides - that is how long it took for him to attain majority rule upon reaching 21 years of age. Until that time, Scottish history was marked by a bitter struggle for regency over the boy-King, by two parties, one led by the Earl of Menteith, Walter Comyn, the other by the Scottish Justiciar, Alan

Durward. However, after many squabbles and bitter struggles, the two parties reached an agreement of co-regency.

As soon as Alexander III became a ruler in his own right, at age 21, he decided to focus on the centuries old issue of the Hebrides - or the Western Isles. His first approach to laying a claim on the island was through sending an official request to the King of Norway, Haakon Haakonsson: his claim was promptly rejected. Alexander III declared to his opponent that he would take the islands by force, if the Norwegians would not sell them. This dispute quickly erupted into an all-out war - the Scottish-Norwegian War of 1262-1266. In response to Alexander's threats, Haakon Haakonsson sailed out of Norway in 1263 at the head of a massive fleet of 120 ships. His initial stop was at the Isle of Arran, where negotiations between the two rulers were to be held. However, Alexander was quick to show his shrewdness and ability as a young and competent monarch. Realizing that this war could be lost if the Norwegians were to win a decisive victory before the onset of winter, Alexander stalled and delayed - allowing autumn to arrive, and with it the fierce storms. Due to this, the stormy weather of approaching winter caused a number of Norwegian ships to become stranded close to the Scottish city of Largs, at the Firth of Clyde. A part of the Norwegian army went ashore to salvage the ships, and at that time the bulk of the Scottish army arrived as well. What ensued was the crucial Battle of Largs, fought on October 2nd, 1263. It was a battle of much confusion: the clash was centered on the birch and was mostly a series of skirmishes. After both sides suffered losses, the Scottish army withdrew, as did the Norwegian army. The result was, for the most part, indecisive, with both sides claiming victory. However, historians agree that the outcome was in many ways a decisive victory for Scotland: the Norwegian army at once retreated to the Orkneys, in order to winter there. During the winter, their King, Haakon Haakonsson, became ill and died. His successor, Magnus Haakonsson, faced with ongoing internal struggles in Norway, as well as with a lack of funding, had to abandon the oversea campaigns and to give in to the Scottish claims.

Did You Know?

Although a part of Scotland today, the Shetland Islands were a part of Norway until 1469. This led to a unique identity of the island, and its own language - the Norn. The settlement of the Vikings, those fierce Norse seafarers, began in Shetland in the 800s. And it was intense, being in such a close proximity to Scandinavian nations and the Faroe Islands. This meant that a Norse presence was much stronger in the Shetlands than elsewhere in Scotland. The Old Norse language was perhaps the only language in these islands and evolved into the distinct Norn. Scholars agree that Norn was used for quite a long time, even after the islands became a part of Scotland. The last living speaker of the Norn language was one Walter Sutherland, living in the northernmost house in the British Isles. When he died in 1850, the language died with him. Isn't it interesting that a form of Old Norse persevered for so long - and in Scotland of all places!?

Just three years after the Battle of Largs, the Norwegians had to sign the Treaty of Perth in 1266. This ended the conflict between the two kingdoms and recognized Scottish sovereignty over the Hebrides - for a one-time payment of 4,000 marks, and an annual payment of 100 marks. In turn, the Scottish King recognized Norwegian sovereignty over Shetland and the Orkneys. Thus ended the old conflict between Norway and Scotland, and the traditionally Gaelic areas of the Inner and Outer Hebrides became an integral part of the Kingdom of Scotland, just as they are today.

A Struggle for Freedom:
Scotland's Wars for Independence

For the most part, the reign of Alexander III was successful, continuing on the achievements of his predecessors, namely David I. He pursued a policy of peace with England and attained the Hebrides for his own realm. However, upon his death in March 1286, Scotland was about to enter into a period of darkness and despair.

Alexander III left this world before his time - by accident. It happened around the time of his second marriage - to Yolande of Dreux, the Countess of Montfort. His first marriage, to Margaret, the daughter of the English King Henry III, ended in 1275, after her death. The two had three children. Alexander's two sons - heirs apparent - both died young, in 1281 and 1284. Their only surviving child was a daughter, Margaret, who was married to King of Norway, Eric II. Thus, in need of a male heir, Alexander married Yolande of Dreux in 1285. In a fateful turn of events, however, Alexander died when traveling to visit his new queen. Wanting to celebrate her birthday on the next day, he traveled at night from Edinburgh to Kinghorn on March 19th, 1286. Numerous warnings were given to him, stating that a horse journey at night, during stormy weather, was highly treacherous. Alexander ignored all warnings, and eventually became separated from his traveling party and lost during the night. His retinue found him in the morning - at the bottom of a cliff and with a broken neck. The King suffered an accident when his horse lost its footing and the two plummeted to their doom. It was an untimely and unfortunate demise for a promising Scottish King. And it was a monumental event for a number of reasons. The foremost of these was the question of a legitimate heir to the Scottish throne, which became vacant so suddenly. Queen Yolande was, in fact, pregnant when the King died, but her child was stillborn. This left only the granddaughter of late

Alexander as a legitimate heiress to the throne. This was, however, a girl of three years, Margaret of Norway. Almost at once, troubles in Scotland erupted. The envoy of the Norwegian King arrived in Scotland promptly, in order to claim the kingdom for the child-queen. At once, the Bruces revolted - and were quickly suppressed in 1287. Realizing the precarious situation, the Norwegian King did not at once dispatch the little girl to Scotland. But when he did so, in 1290, disaster struck - as the seven-year-old Margaret died soon after arriving at Orkney, likely from food poisoning and frail health. Soon after she died, 13 claimants for the Scottish throne stepped forward - all wanting to rule. Trouble was almost guaranteed.

The following list, derived from the famous Burke's Royal Peerage, gives us a great insight into the 13 claimants and their ties to the Scottish throne. Here, we quote it directly:

"•*John Balliol, Lord of Galloway, son of Devorguilla, daughter of Margaret, eldest daughter of David, Earl of Huntingdon, son of Henry, Earl of Huntingdon, son of King David I. He pleaded primogeniture in a legitimate, cognatic line.*

•*Robert de Brus, 5th Lord of Annandale, son of Isabella, second daughter of David, Earl of Huntingdon. This Robert Bruce was regent of Scotland sometime during the minority of King Alexander III and was occasionally recognized as a tanist of the Scottish throne. In the succession dispute, he pleaded tanistry and proximity in degree of kinship to the previous monarch, his descent being a generation shorter.*

•*John Hastings, 1st Baron Hastings, son of Henry de Hastings, son of Ada, third daughter of David, Earl of Huntingdon.*

•*Floris V, Count of Holland, son of William II, Count of Holland, son of Floris IV, Count of Holland, son of William I, Count of Holland, son of Ada, daughter of Henry, Earl of Huntingdon. He claimed that David,*

Earl of Huntingdon, had renounced his hereditary rights to the throne of Scotland.

•John "the Black" Comyn, Lord of Badenoch, son of John Comyn, son of Richard Comyn, son of William Comyn, son of Hextilda, daughter of Bethóc, daughter of King Donald III.

•Nicholas de Soules, son of Ermengarde, daughter of Marjorie, natural daughter of King Alexander II. •Patrick Galithly, son of Henry Galithly, natural son of King William the Lion.

•William de Ros, 1st Baron de Ros, son of Robert de Ros, son of William de Ros of Hamlake, son of Isabella, natural daughter of King William the Lion.

•William de Vesci, Baron de Vesci, son of William de Vesci, son of Margaret, illegitimate daughter of King William the Lion.

•Patrick Dunbar, 7th Earl of Dunbar, son of Patrick, 6th Earl of Dunbar, son of Patrick, 5th Earl of Dunbar, son of Ada, natural daughter of King William the Lion.

•Roger de Mandeville, son of Agatha, daughter of Aufrica, daughter of William de Say, son of Aufrica, natural daughter of King William the Lion.

•Robert de Pinkeney, son of Henry, son of Alicia, daughter of Marjorie, an alleged natural daughter of Henry, Earl of Huntingdon.

•Eric II, King of Norway, father of Queen Margaret and son-in-law of King Alexander III."

With the conflict over the succession almost inevitable, the leading men of Scotland had to come to a decision - and fast. With Yolande of Dreux still pregnant, it was possible (at the time) that the late King Alexander III would be in fact presented with an (infant) male heir.

Until that happened, however, the realm had to be governed. To that end, seven special "Guardians" of the Kingdom were appointed to rule together. These "custodians of the realm" were gathered from the leading Scottish nobles and clergymen, appointed in near-equal numbers: three bishops, two barons, and two earls. They were considered as effective representatives of the political community of the whole realm. These guardians were: Robert Wishart, Bishop of Glasgow; William, the Bishop of Dunkeld; William Fraser, the Bishop of St. Andrews; Alexander Comyn, Earl of Buchan; Duncan, the Earl of Fife; John Comyn, Lord of Badenoch; and James the Steward, the famed ancestor of the later Stuart Kings. In many ways, this appointment of the seven leading men of Scotland can be seen as a reflection of the unity of the nation's nobility, even though such a unity was shaky at best. Nevertheless, history showed us that on many other occasions, in different countries and kingdoms - England for example -, such vacancies at the throne and the troubles of succession almost at once led to open civil warfare. Scotland's leading men thus showed a good deal of honor and commitment to the Royal line, even though there were pretenders to the throne and those who opposed them.

One of the most vocal claimants to the Scottish throne was Robert the Bruce, fifth of his name. The Bruces (all bearing the name Robert, which might be confusing) were one of the most prominent families of Scotland, tracing their early origins to the Norman conquest of the British Isles and the Norman noble family of "de Bruis". Their claim was legitimate, however, as Robert Bruce, the 5th Lord of Annandale, was one of the great-great-grandsons of the famed King David I. Around the time of these events, the Bruce family held power in Southwest Scotland, and held many estates in England as well.

The next claimant to the throne with an equally legitimate cause was a somewhat hitherto unknown nobleman - John Balliol. For the Scottish nobility, this man was a sort of newcomer, having spent a good deal of his life at estates across England and France. Balliol was the heir of the great Lordship of Galloway as well, through his mother. As we saw from Burke's lineage, John Balliol had the luck to be the son of Lady Dervorguilla of Galloway, herself the granddaughter of David, Earl of Huntingdon - the brother of the ex-Scottish King William the Lion. As such, he had a very strong claim to the throne. Furthermore, he was - through marriage - related to one of the most powerful noble families in Scotland - the Comyns. Key political players, the Comyns held many lands in Scotland, and no less than two of their family were appointed as Guardians of Scotland. Two branches existed, senior and junior, held by Lord of Badenoch and the Earl of Buchan respectively.

And so it was that - of all the 13 (14 in some sources) claimants - the Bruce and the Balliol had the strongest claims of all. The two began gathering their own supporters, as they were the likeliest to (eventually) ascend to the throne. Robert the Bruce met with a number of his close supporters, amongst whom was the powerful James the Steward. They held a meeting at Turnberry Castle, the seat of the Earls of Carrick, where they created the "Turnberry Band", a pact that supported Bruce's claim to the throne. Two prominent Irish lords were also a part of the deal: Thomas de Clare and Richard de Burgh. Likewise, supporters of Balliol's claim also gathered around him. This - in the views of many - posed a significant threat of civil war in Scotland. And, when the child of Alexander's widow Yolande proved to be stillborn, with no heir produced, the Bruces were quick to act. They proclaimed their cause throughout Annandale and have occupied some castles held by the Balliols. But they lacked crucial support on a wider scale and were quickly forced to seek terms with the "Guardians of Scotland". The Bruces now had to bide their time.

Did You Know?

The American 1995 movie, "Braveheart", deals with the life and exploits of the famed Scottish hero, William Wallace. The movie served to introduce the historic background of the Scottish Wars for Independence to the wider audience and general public, presenting it in a more engaging, and heroic way. It became one of Hollywood's most successful movies, grossing a total of $213.2 million against a budget of $70 million. Receiving numerous accolades and rewards, such as five Academy Awards, three BAFTA awards, and one Golden Globe, it helped to attract the general public to the history of medieval Scotland. And although the script for the movie was based on the medieval epic poem by Blind Harry, "The Wallace", it was still, however, a Hollywood blockbuster. This meant that many historical inaccuracies exist in the movie. Nevertheless, it remains one of the foremost screen depictions of William Wallace and his heroic exploits in Scotland's First War for Independence.

Enter the English King, Edward I - the Longshanks. Ever hungry for the rugged lands of Alba, the English monarch observed the unfolding events with great care. However - oddly enough - it was the Scots that came to him, rather than he to them. Fearing that a bloody civil war was on the brink, the Guardians of Scotland, after weighing all their options following hours of debate, decided to turn to the English King for "counsel and protection". In simplest terms, they wanted him to act as an arbitrator in the situation, especially after the unexpected and untimely death of the young Margaret of Norway. The Scottish representatives wrote to Edward, urging him to "travel swiftly north", for the "consolation of the Scottish people and for preventing the shedding of blood". However, the ambitious King of England had more in mind than just simple arbitration. In early 1291, he emerged from a somewhat reclusive winter spent in Ashridge Priory, where he mourned the death of his wife that struck him deeply. After emerging following the winter, he supposedly declared that *it was in his mind to reduce the king and kingdom of Scotland to his rule, as he had recently subjected Wales to his authority".*

King Edward and the Guardians of Scotland met in Norham in May 1291. Before any agreement could be reached, however, Edward insisted that the Scottish representatives recognize him as the Lord Paramount of Scotland. Edward made sure to find and pursue his rights to the claim of overlordship of Scotland, threatening an invasion if the Guardians would not comply. He gave them three weeks to reconsider, after they refused initially. It was a well-played ploy by Edward. He knew quite well that a military invasion of Scotland would come at a bad moment for the latter, and he also knew that the Scottish Guardians all had vast estates in England - estates that they would surely lose if it came to war. Thus, in many ways, he forced the Scottish nobles to recognize him as the Lord Paramount of Scotland, so that he could arbitrate in their matters. What ensued was the "Great Cause", a lengthy and quite complex legal process that would decide the future ruler of Scotland. All the while, the English King - who would be later known as the Hammer of the Scots - exerted his overlordship over Scotland and expanded his realm further, retaining the Isle of Man and occupying key Scottish castles. It was a very fragile situation, no doubt, where a delicate peace was maintained for over a year. Edward effectively took over Scotland without even a sword being drawn, cunningly and - some would say - treacherously. And the grudges and animosity amongst the Scottish nobles could not be overlooked. Nevertheless, Edward Longshanks approached his decision of the future Scottish monarch with great care, taking the pleas of all 14 claimants with all seriousness. Just the two of the claims, however, were truly reasonable - that of Robert Bruce and of John Balliol. After much consideration, and a lengthy court process, King Edward at last decided that it was the claim of John Balliol that was the winning one - as he was after all, the rightful claimant by right of *primogeniture*. On November 17th, 1292, Edward declared that Balliol was the new king.

It has to be noted that King Edward, after John Balliol was crowned at Scone, did right by Scotland - and remember the rights of others. He allowed the new Scottish monarch to take back the Scottish castles (and the realm as a whole). However, he made sure that it was still known that the English King was - in the end - the overlord of Scotland. To that end, King John Balliol had to travel to Newcastle to pay homage to Edward, whereupon he addressed him as "Lord Edward, Lord superior of the Realm of Scotland" and became his "liegeman". Thus, once again, Scotland lost its independence, falling once more under the mercies of England.

Still, many disliked the newly developed situation. Things got heated up especially in mid-1294, when Edward demanded that King John Balliol had until September of that year to provide him with fresh troops and funds for England's invasion of France. It was becoming clear that King Edward saw Scotland as a mere vassal of his, and the situation became unbearable for the Scottish nobility. When Balliol returned to Scotland after a meeting with the English King, a heated meeting was held, where plans were made to openly defy Edward. King John Balliol was to be advised by a newly created war council, made up of 12 members total - four bishops, four barons, and four earls. It was clear that Edward would not tolerate defiance, and that an invasion from England was unavoidable. The Scottish wisely used this opportunity to strengthen their alliance with the French - emissaries were sent almost at once, informing the French King of Edward's plans for invasion. The Scots also gave guarantees of conducting attacks on England in the case of the latter's invasion of France. In return, of course, Scotland would have French support - no small thing. The alliance between Scotland and France - known as the Auld Alliance, would last intermittently until the mid-1500s.

By 1296, it was becoming clear that a war between the two kingdoms was inevitable. Edward suspected an invasion, especially after learning of the secret negotiations between France and Scotland. To that end, he began forming a militia and strengthened his possessions along the Scottish border, amassing troops there. King John Balliol was aware of these troop movements, to which he responded by ordering all able-bodied Scotsmen to bear arms and assemble for war. All the while, the animosity between John Balliol and Robert the Bruce deepened, and the latter chose to completely ignore the summons by the King. Either way, what ensued is one of the principal episodes of the history of Scotland, the First War of Scottish Independence, a brief struggle that opened up the Wars of Scottish Independence as a whole. In simplest terms, these wars were fought to keep Scotland free of English rule.

In many ways, John Balliol was a weak and ineffectual king, delivering no crucial decisions on his own, seen by the English as a common vassal lord and not much more. In just a few years, Scotland was reduced to a vassal state from the prosperous and bountiful reign of Alexander III. Due to all this, John Balliol was commonly known as "Toom Tabard", translated to "Empty Coat", likely due to his ineffective reign, or perhaps due to his simple (empty) coat of arms. Either way, pressured by the rest of the Scottish nobles and the custodians, King John denounced his homage to Edward Longshanks in March of 1296. It was in that same month that Edward responded by invading Scotland. At the onset of his military campaign, Edward attacked and sacked the prosperous Scottish town of Berwick-upon-Tweed, which was situated on the border between the two realms. Contemporary accounts documented the viciousness of the English assault: between 4,000 and 17,000 civilians were reportedly slaughtered by the English troops. One account gives us a ghastly report:

"When the town had been taken in this way and its citizens had submitted, Edward spared no one, whatever the age or sex, and for two days streams of blood flowed from the bodies of the slain, for in his

tyrannous rage he ordered 7,500 souls of both sexes to be massacred.... So that mills could be turned by the flow of their blood."

Around this time, the first famed patriots of Scotland arose in revolt. These were the famed William Wallace and Andrew de Moray. William Wallace was one of the first to conduct actions and campaigns against the English, rising to prominence in mid-1297 after he conducted the Action at Lanark, whereupon his men killed the Sheriff of Lanark and defeated his forces. The news of this victory resounded across the Highlands, and men quickly flocked to William Wallace's side and his cause. Soon after, Wallace gained recognition and the blessing of Robert Wishart, the Bishop of Glasgow. This gave him the necessary credibility and strengthened his cause. Edward Longshanks termed the insurrections as the "Scottish Problem" and was keen to deal with it swiftly. Around this time, a significant event took place. Edward Longshanks dispatched his servant, Robert Bruce, the Earl of Carrick, to deal with Wallace and the others who flocked to him. But Bruce had a change of heart en-route and decided to band together with his Scottish brethren instead of serving the English King. He reportedly said: "No man holds his flesh and blood in hatred, and I am no exception. I must join my own people and the nation in whom I was born."

Soon afterwards, the first major battle of this early war occurred. This was the Battle of Stirling Bridge, fought on September 11th, 1297, where the Scottish forces under William Wallace faced off against the English under the command of the Earl of Surrey, John de Warenne. A ferocious battle, it displayed the ineffective command by the English and the cunning deployment of the Scottish forces. Commanding the better grounds across the River Forth, the Scots waited for the English to cross the very narrow bridge - the only ford across the water. With the bridge being so narrow, it took the English a long time to cross, and the Scots waited in hiding. When the time was right, Wallace ordered the assault - and it came swiftly and fiercely. With careful maneuvering, the Scottish troops managed to cut off the approach of English reinforcements and proceeded to outright slaughter the English troops that were cut off after crossing the bridge. The rest of the English army could do naught but observe the carnage from across the river, realizing the mistake that was made in ordering the troops to cross. The idea was put forward by one of the aides of the Earl of Surrey, one Sir Hugh de Cressingham. The latter was greatly hated by the Scots, due to his alleged practice of flaying Scottish prisoners. It was William Wallace himself that defeated Cressingham in battle and proceeded to flay him. Accounts state that - in revenge - Wallace made a baldric (shoulder-worn belt) out of the dried skin of Hugh de Cressingham. In unison with the attack at Stirling Bridge, the English supply trains in the rear were also attacked, causing further losses amongst the English. In the end, realizing the battle was utterly lost, the Earl of Surrey fled towards the plundered Berwick. The Battle of Stirling was a cunning and decisive Scottish victory, and a great boost for their morale.

An Age of Strife and Turmoil

Alas, the joy of the Scots was not to last long: just one year later, King Edward himself rode out into Scotland to face the "threat", as he so put it. Following their victory at Stirling Bridge, the Scots were keen to capitalize on that win: they rode southwards into England, raiding and plundering, from Carlisle to Newcastle. But Edward was not going to let that go unchecked. He returned from his trip to France, and immediately set about gathering a sizable army. On July 21st, 1298, he had penetrated as far as Falkirk, where he chanced upon the Scottish army, led by their hero, William Wallace. Without hesitation, Edward ordered an attack on the following day. This resulted in the famed Battle of Falkirk, in which the 15,000-strong English army faced the Scots of William Wallace who numbered just 6,000 men. It was a ruthless, and one-sided clash. The Scottish army was arrayed into four great "schiltrons", an offensive formation resembling "hedgehogs" full of long spears. When the English cavalry charged these formations, it made no effect - the spears held them at bay and caused great casualties. However, these spearman formations were poorly defended from other attacks. Edward knew this and quickly brought in his slingers and archers - all in great numbers. When they began raining down arrows and projectiles onto the undefended Scottish formations - the end was guaranteed. As the Scottish casualties mounted, and their lines wavered, a final push by the English cavalry and infantry at last broke them, causing the survivors to flee and bringing an end to the battle. It was a decisive English victory, with both sides suffering some 2,000 casualties each.

Following this defeat, William Wallace's military reputation greatly suffered. He was still hailed as a folk hero, known for his early rise to arms against the English, and his initial successes in battles. However, it needs to be noted that much of the pomp and fame surrounding

William Wallace was not present in his own time, but only arose in generations that followed. In fact, much that is known of William Wallace's exploits comes from the Scottish poet, Blind Harry, who wrote his works some 200 years after Wallace's time. He wrote much of the tales in order to entertain King James, during his reign between 1488 and 1513, and used many embellishments. To that end, modern historians considered that Blind Harry's accounts of William Wallace are part fact, and part fiction. Either way, following the devastating defeat at the Battle of Falkirk, not much was known about Wallace's whereabouts. But by 1305, some 7 years after that defeat, he was once again in Scotland. In that same year, he was betrayed to the English and was captured. He was promptly tried for his alleged atrocities against civilians, and for treason also. During his trial, William Wallace famously stated: "I could not be a traitor to Edward, for I was never his subject." Either way, unjustly sentenced, the Scottish hero William Wallace was executed on August 23rd, 1305, in his 35-th year. His death was most atrocious, designed to bring him much suffering.

"And afterwards for the measureless wickedness which he did to God and to the most Holy Church by burning churches, vessels and shrines, in which the body of Christ and the bodies of the saints and relics of the same were wont to be placed together, the heart, liver, and lung and all the internal [parts] of the same William, by which such evil thoughts proceeded, should be dispatched to the fire and burned. And also because he had committed both murders and felonies, not only to the lord the King himself but to the entire people of England and Scotland, the body of that William should be cut up and divided and cut up into four quarters, and that the head thus cut off should be affixed upon London bridge in the sight of those crossing both by land and by water, and one quarter should be hung on the gibbet at Newcastle upon Tyne, another quarter at Berwick, a third quarter at Stirling, and a fourth quarter at St John's town [Perth] as a cause of fear and chastisement of all going past and looking upon these things."

Such was the extent of the English hate towards him. First, he was stripped naked and dragged through the city behind a horse. Then, at the execution place, he was strangled - but not killed - and, while still alive, he was first emasculated (privates cut off), then disemboweled, with his intestines burned before his eyes, and only then was he beheaded and cut into four parts. This utterly cruel method of execution was not new to the English. In fact, it was one of their staples, being known as "hanged, drawn, and quartered". The four body parts of Wallace were displayed for all to see in Berwick, Newcastle, Perth, and Stirling, while his preserved head was displayed atop the London Bridge. The English, through their unnecessarily cruel murder, wanted to crush the Scottish spirits, and to show them that with the severed head of William Wallace, the fighting zeal of the Scots was also cut off. But it was not: in fact, the martyr's death of William Wallace only served to strengthen the Scottish cause, further fueling the flame of their freedom fight.

Following Falkirk, however, the early stage of the Scottish War for Independence slowly petered out. The fighting spirit was there, to be certain, but had to be kept for another time. King Edward continued his campaigns, but never subdued Scotland entirely. By 1304, Scotland's strongest and most important castle - Stirling Castle - was finally captured by the English after a long siege. This resulted in negotiations between the two parties, leading to most of the Scottish nobles to swear homage to Edward. And with the cruel death of William Wallace in the following year, it seemed that the Scots were all but defeated, and the initial revolt came to an end. It is usually known as the First War of Scottish Independence, but the Scots could not be calmed. Their struggle would soon continue, fueled by the need for a Scottish King, and that elusive, much sought-after freedom. In 1306, at the meeting between the last two claimants of the Scottish throne: Robert the Bruce, and John Comyn, in a heated argument, the Bruce murdered John Comyn at the Greyfriars Kirk in Dumfries, thus removing his sole competitor for the throne. Allegedly, Bruce's party discovered documents that implicated a planned treason by Comyn, who wanted to betray Bruce to the English in order to become King. Either way, Robert the Bruce was now alone in the race for the throne. He quickly gathered all the nobles and the clergy behind him, and no more than five weeks after Comyn's death, he was crowned the new King of Scots - lawfully and uncontested.

At once began a new struggle for Scotland's freedom and independence from the English. On June 19th, 1306, King Robert the Bruce suffered his first initial setback, being defeated by the English at the Battle of Methven, where he faced the forces of Aymer de Valence, 2nd Earl of Pembroke. Bruce was outnumbered and taken by surprise and stood no chance against the English. Notably, King Edward I gave strict orders that any Scottish soldier or noble who was captured was to be "given no quarter", and to be given no mercy, to be executed without trial. This was due to his rage at Robert the Bruce's "betrayal" and rise to arms. As a result of this policy, several leading Scottish nobles that were captured at the battle were later executed, including Alexander Scrymgeour, Hugh de la Haye, and others.

Following Methven, Edward I declared Robert the Bruce an outlaw. But in 1307, his time had come to an end. While on campaign, King Edward caught dysentery. By July of that year, he was severely emaciated and weak, and when his servants picked him up to feed him one morning, he simply died in their arms. It was a turning point for the Scots, no doubt. The notorious "Hammer of the Scots" died, and this gave further fuel to the Scottish freedom fight. Supporters began to rally behind Robert the Bruce, and his forces continued to grow stronger and stronger. In time, successes of the Scottish army began to roll one behind another. Ground was being reclaimed, with a major victory at the Battle of Loudoun Hill, where Bruce avenged himself on Aymer de Valence.

Next was the Battle of Brander Pass, and the recapture of Edinburgh and Roxburgh Castles. The English were slowly losing their iron grip on Scotland. And this string of successes culminated in 1314, with one of the decisive events in the whole of Scottish history - the Battle of Bannockburn. Fought on June 23-24th 1314, it was a culminating event. In that year, the new and young English King Edward II, invaded Scotland at the head of a truly massive army, one of the largest to ever enter this nation. This he did in order to relieve the besieged Stirling Castle, a key strategic position. This army numbered some 25,000 infantry and 2,000 cavalry, meant to face a Scottish army of just 6,000 men. The two forces soon squared off in one fated duel.

Did You Know?

The modern notion of the traditional kilts and tartans as worn by the Highland clansmen is largely a product of the 19th century romanticizing of the classic Highlander of history. Before this time, tartan colors were not associated with a specific clan, as they are today, and a different color could only be linked to a different region of the Highlands. However, following the 1822 visit of King George IV to Scotland, whereupon he wore a fashionable kilt, this piece of highland clothing became extremely popular once again. In fact, the demand for kilts was so high at the time, that the entire Scottish linen industry could not keep up with the demand. However, the appearance of the modern kilt with all its fancy fittings is a stark contrast to the kilt of the past centuries. The so-called "belted plaid", or simply "plaid", was an invaluable asset for any highlander, as it could serve as a cloak, a blanket, pillow, cowl, and many other things besides. In comparison, modern kilts are much smaller, shorter, and used for a ceremonial purpose at best.

Bruce decided to divide his small army into three separate contingents, and to prevent the errors used by William Wallace by using his schiltron formations in an offensive role. The first day of the battle was marked by a legendary duel in the midst of the raging clash. In the duel, Robert the Bruce squared off against the young knight Sir Henry de Bohun. In an almost legendary episode, Bruce split Bohun's head with an ax and thus bolstered the Scottish morale with his feat. The battle's turning point was the defection of a Scottish noble, Sir Alexander Seton. He served the English but rejoined his Scottish kindred and gave them crucial information of the enemy's positions and the low morale of their army. Hearing of this, Robert the Bruce decided to launch a devastating and unreserved all-out attack on the English camp. What ensued was a decisive decimation of the English troops that were hemmed in against the Bannockburn. With their cavalry unable to maneuver, and their archers unable to shoot at the Scots (because they'd shoot their own men), it was pretty much a sealed fate for the English. The seasoned battle veterans such as Aymer de Valence and Giles d'Argentan quickly understood their position, and promptly led King Edward II to safety. Giles d'Argentan was at the time considered the third best knight in the world - a man of incredible prowess and courage. Upon leading the King to safety, he told him: "Sire, your protection was committed to me, but since you are safely on your way, I will bid you farewell for never yet have I fled from a battle, nor will I now." He wheeled his horse back and returned to the battle, charging the Scottish troops where he was overwhelmed and killed in battle. This was not the only prominent English noble to fall at Bannockburn - there were many who became casualties, such as the Earl of Gloucester, William Marshal, John de Montfort, Sir Robert Clifford, and others.

As a result of their crushing defeat at Bannockburn, the English suffered some 11,000 infantrymen killed, being ground-up meticulously by the advancing Scottish schiltrons. On the other hand, Scottish losses in the battle were incredibly low, owing to their surprise attack, and their advantageous positions. Undoubtedly, Bannockburn was a pivotal event in Scottish history. It was the last push to expel the English. That push was finalized with the recapture of Berwick in 1318. In 1320, the formalization of Scottish independence continued. In that year, the Scots created the Declaration of Arbroath, a formal document affirming their independence from the English, sealed by more than 50 Scottish nobles.

"As long as only one hundred of us remain alive we will never on any conditions be brought under English rule. For we fight not for glory, nor riches, nor honors, but for Freedom alone, which no good man gives up except with his life." - excerpt from the Declaration of Arbroath

From here, successes only continued for the Scots. In 1327, Edward II was deposed and killed, with his son Edward III taking up his place. In that very same year, the newly crowned King marched northwards to face the Scottish armies that had been raiding into English territories. This resulted in the July-August Battle of Stanhope Park, another decisive Scottish victory in which Edward III very nearly evaded capture - a thing that would be utterly fatal for the English. In the end, the English understood that Scotland could not be subdued so easily. Edward III was forced to sign the Treaty of Edinburgh-Northampton on May 1st, 1328, with which he formally recognized Scotland's independence and Robert the Bruce as King of Scots.

The Second Scottish War for Independence

However, the troubles were soon to resume, with the start of the Second Scottish War for Independence, which formally lasted from 1332 to 1357. King Robert the Bruce died in 1329, aged just 55. It was apparent that he suffered from an undisclosed illness for quite a number of years and would at last perish from it while still in his prime years. He was succeeded by his son and heir David II, who was still way too young to rule. It was the Earl of Moray, Thomas Randolph, who assumed custody of the boy, as per Robert's wishes. However, Edward III was not keen on letting his defeat go so easily and was quick to capitalize on the death of Robert the Bruce. He felt humiliated and wanted to avenge himself on the Scots. He also had the assistance and the allegiance of a number of Scottish nobles, chiefly of Edward Balliol, son of the ex-king John Balliol, who appeared as a claimant to the throne. Furthermore, a number of nobles that opposed Bruce, and were thus stripped of their lands and castles, flocked to Edward's side in order to return their lost lands. It was, after all, these treacherous Scottish nobles that led to the undoing of the peace treaty and the renewed threat of the English.

Having gained the support of Edward III, Edward Balliol assembled a small army and landed at Kinghorn in Scotland. However, the Scots learned of their arrival and assembled a massive army near Perth. The two forces met in the Battle of Dupplin Moor on August 11th, 1332, the first clash of the Second War of Independence. For a first glance, everything was set for a crushing Scottish victory; after all, they had between 15,000 and 40,000 men assembled, compared to just 1,500 assembled by Edward Balliol. Alas, disaster struck. The Battle of Dupplin Moor was a crushing Scottish defeat, a result of their inadvertent entrapment in a narrow valley. Their forces were tightly packed together, unable to maneuver or even use their weapons. All the while, English archers pummeled them from the sides. The battle was disastrous, and many Scottish nobles died as a result. Edward Balliol proceeded victorious to Perth, where he crowned himself the new King of Scots. Edward III, King of England, at once reacted to these news by moving his own armies northward into Scotland.

By mid-1333, the English and Balliol together laid siege to Berwick, one of Scotland's foremost towns. However, the Scottish, led by the new guardian of the realm, Archibald Douglas, rushed in an attempt to relieve the siege. This resulted in the Battle of Halidon Hill, fought on July 19th, 1333. This clash was an absolute and utter disaster for the Scottish - one that was not seen for centuries before or after. Their assault on the English positions utterly failed: the English had favorable defensive positions, and their longbowmen ravaged the approaching Scots, claiming many lives. The infantry then entered the fray, and the pummeled Scots soon broke and fled in full retreat. Then the English cavalry mounted up and pursued them for many miles, slaying thousands. In the end, an estimated 10,000 Scots were killed in the battle. In comparison, just 7 to 14 English casualties were documented. It was an event never before witnessed. Douglas, and five more most important and senior Scottish nobles were dead, and also countless nobles and knights. The string of Scottish successes came to an abrupt and heart wrenching halt.

Berwick was soon annexed by Edward III, and much of Scotland's Lowland ceded to England as well. For the next couple of years, Scotland was pushed into a whirlwind of chaos and struggle: the independent and recognized nation nhat Robert the Bruce won so incredibly hard, was now shattered into pieces and fought over, inch by inch. The new Guardian of Scotland, Sir Andrew Murray, rose to lead the tattered Scottish forces that were still loyal to the heritage of Robert the Bruce. Together, they led a guerrilla warfare struggle against Balliol and his supporters, refusing to let go of the Scottish "freedom fighting spirit". Gathering at the historic Dumbarton Castle, Andrew Murray and his followers - Earls of Ross and March, William Douglas, Lord of Liddesdale, William Keith, Maurice Murray, and others - they all formed the "nucleus of the [Scottish] national revival". The two opposing sides struggling for Scotland - the Bruce and Balliol supporters - clashed in November 1335 at the Battle of Culblean, which was a decisive and important victory for Andrew Murray. It finally broke the attempts of Edward Balliol to usurp the Scottish throne - he was deposed in 1336.

This victory was a bit of a "breath of fresh air" that the Scottish people needed, the Bruce loyalists. It turned the favor of this new war ever so slightly in their favor. But even so, the nation was in need of stability and a strong king. The economy that was established by Robert the Bruce was decimated, hundreds of the leading, veteran nobles were dead, and the country was aflame. In 1341, the heir of Robert the Bruce, David II, now some 17-18 years old, at last returned to Scotland from exile - determined to live up to the glory of his late father. It was now his chance to finally wrest Alba from the hands of the pretenders: he was ambitious, strong, and heeded the advice of Andrew Murray and the rest. Also, a contributing factor was the beginning of the Hundred Years' War between England and France, which prevented the English King from fully investing his forces in England.

By 1346, the recovered Scottish realm led a series of raids into England - a response to the French King who asked for such a diversion to lighten the English pressures on Calais, in France. Young David II accepted, and penetrated deep into the north of England. There, however, disaster struck again, when the Scots were met by the English in the Battle of Neville's Cross, on October 17th, 1346. Young David II was surprised, and his army - although numerically superior, was crushed. As a result, most of the Scottish leadership - their seasoned commanders and nobles - were either dead or captured, which essentially left Scotland without efficient leadership. But worse than this was the capture of the King himself, David II. During the battle he was wounded in the face by two arrows. He fled and hid beneath a bridge, where passing English soldiers saw his reflection in the water, promptly capturing him. The wounds were, miraculously, not mortal. One arrowhead was removed from his face, while the other remained lodged in it permanently, causing many headaches throughout his life. King David II was imprisoned in England for the next 11 years. During this time, Scotland was governed by Robert II, son of Walter Stewart and his wife Marjorie, herself a daughter of Robert the Bruce.

After 11 long years, David II finally got the chance to return to Scotland as its rightful King. Under the Treaty of Berwick, the Scots were allowed to ransom their King for the sum of 100,000 merks (Scottish silver coins), to be paid in yearly installments of 10,000 merks. This was an enormous sum for the time, but the Scottish agreed. However, it was soon clear that the agreement could not be kept. Scotland was at the time in an utterly sorry state. It was ravaged by constant warfare, its economy in shambles, devoid of capable leaders and nobles, and on top of that - affected by the Black Death. After managing to pay the first installment of 10,000 on time, they were late with the second installment, and could not even collect enough money for the third. However, this was later ironed out, partially by secret negotiations between David and Edward, and the situation of England's much more important war with France. In the end, a sum of 24,000 merks was never paid to England.

During the reign of David II - which was not all that popular in Scotland - the economy began to reel back somewhat, although the nation was still in a very poor state. However, from 1357 and the Treaty of Berwick, it was again an independent nation - and that was well worth the poverty.

David II died in 1371, aged 46, during the height of his power. David's rule was going in a good direction of prosperity. Scotland was beginning to recover, getting back on its feet. But alas, death struck unexpectedly. David II was the last male of the House of Bruce, and was succeeded to the throne by Robert II, his nephew and the first Scottish monarch from the House of Stewart. Robert held the throne efficiently, although coming to rule at age 55. During his reign the entirety of occupied Scottish lands were reclaimed, and power was consolidated once more. However, he died in 1390, aged 74, and the rule passed to his son, Robert III Stewart.

Robert III was somewhat frail and of fragile health. The real power at the time was in the hands of his own brother, the Duke of Albany - also named Robert. The Duke of Albany was noted as a ruthless politician who did anything for power. Thus, it was, that King Robert III's eldest son and heir, David, mysteriously died - and the finger of suspicion pointed towards none other than the Duke of Albany. Fearing further deaths, King Robert III sent his younger son, James I, to exile in France. However, in a tragic turn of events, young James was captured by the English and spent the next 18 years as their prisoner. During that time, and following the death of King Robert III Steward, Scotland was ruled by regents - of course they were the Duke of Albany, and later his son, Murdoch Stewart.

A New Era:
The Coming of the Stuarts

James I, the heir of the Scottish Crown, now returned to Scotland in 1424, aged 32. He was ready to reassert his rule in the nation, and to wrest the Dukes of Albany out of power. He killed Murdoch Stewart and his sons and continued with the detainment of several key Scottish nobles. He did this in order to centralize his rule - a risky move that caused him to become very unpopular. In the end, he was assassinated in a failed coup attempt in 1437. His wife, however, managed to escape with their son - now king - James II, a boy of six.

Young James II continued his father's policies, suppressing the individual power of the noble families, such as the Douglases, one of the foremost nobles of the times of Robert the Bruce. James II is regarded in history as a successful Scottish King - being well liked by the common folk and known for his solid legislatures. However, his reign had one major stain upon it - the murder of William Douglas, 8th Earl of Douglas, a powerful magnate whose power James wanted to curb. During a heated discussion, King James II fell into a fit of rage and subsequently stabbed William Douglas repeatedly, for 26 times. Another court official then "struck the man's brains out with an ax", before his body was thrown out of a window. Either way, James II was noted as an ambitious and energetic ruler, whose reign ended way too prematurely. During the Siege of Roxburgh Castle - one of the last castles that was occupied by the English - a cannon that was employed by the Scots accidentally blew up and the resulting explosion killed King James II.

Following his death, the throne was inherited by his young son, James III, a boy of roughly nine. For that reason, his minority was marked by a number of regents that ruled in his stead. However, his later reign was marked with one notable event that must be mentioned for the overall history of Scotland. And that is the acquisition of the Orkneys and of Shetland. This was achieved through his marriage to Princess Margaret of Denmark, and Scotland achieved its greatest territorial expanse ever. Until this day, the Orkneys and Shetland Islands remain an inseparable part of Scotland, as they had always been traditionally. However, a noted trace of the Viking and Norwegian influences can still be observed in dialects and place names.

James III was, in most aspects, a hugely unpopular and disliked monarch. A number of his "odd" and unfavorable policies were hugely disliked by the court, and he even feuded with his wife and his son. Some of the accusations against him were hoarding of money, failure to resolve domestic feuds, as well as an unpopular policy of securing an alliance with England - by that point a hated enemy of the Scots. This situation culminated in 1482, when his brother, Alexander, the Duke of Albany, attempted to usurp the Scottish throne - with the help of none other than the English. This led to a short-lived invasion of Scotland by the English, in July 1482. This invasion lasted for only a month, but nonetheless it had significant consequences upon the flow of Scotland's history at the time. As a result, Berwick-Upon-Tweed, one of the most significant Scottish towns, was captured by the English - and had remained in their hands ever since. The intentions of the Duke of Albany, however, did not come to fruition, and he soon after died in a tourney duel.

James III's unpopularity was destined to be his damnation. He died in the Battle of Sauchieburn near Stirling, on June 11th, 1488, which was an integral part of the second rebellion against his reign. His main opponent was none other than his own son, also named James, who would come out of the battle as the new Scottish King - James IVth.

The Stuart dynasty, in many ways, was instrumental in shaping up the future of Scotland as we know it today. One significant event occurred during the 25-year long reign of King James IV, which would largely usher Scotland into a wholly new era of a union with England. And that event was the marriage of James IV and Margaret Tudor, the daughter of the English King Henry VII, in 1503. Just one hundred years later, the Union of the Crowns would come to pass, when the great-grandson of James IV, James VI, became the King following the death of the English Queen Elizabeth I.

Although the reigns of the Stuart Kings in Scotland might sound rife with instability, internal disputes, and conflicts, they were in fact quite prosperous for the overall development of Scotland. Let us not forget that the nation was still reeling from the very turbulent Wars of Scottish Independence that left the land battle-scarred, its leadership and nobility decimated, and the economy ruined. But by the time of James IV Stuart, a new era of prosperity was arriving step by step. Scotland went alongside the developments in Europe, and the Renaissance first began arriving in the early 1500s. Education was also promoted on a large scale, first time for this nation. Admirable universities were established St. Andrews in 1413, Glasgow in 1450, and Aberdeen in 1495. Also, during the reign of James IV, in 1496, the Education Act was delivered, suggesting that all sons of nobles and freeholders should attend "grammar school." Scotland also expanded during this time, as James IV finally reasserted the royal influence over the semi-independent Lord of the Isles, in the Hebrides. And with the royal rule affirmed throughout Scotland, education and culture were able to reach every place of the nation. James IV also renewed the so-called "Auld Alliance", the alliance with France, upon which he acted in 1512 by invading England as a way to support France. However, the Scottish campaign ended in disaster: at the famed Battle of Flodden Field, the bulk of the Scottish nobility, as well as King James IV, lost their lives. James IV was the last of Scotland's monarchs to have died in battle, and in fact, the last monarch in the British Isles to give his life thus. His untimely death meant that he was to be succeeded by his infant son, King James V. A number of regents would subsequently rule in the boy's stead, until he came of age. And no matter how successful the reigns of the Stuarts were, they were often marred by the untimely deaths of the monarchs, rarely leaving a mature heir to the throne.

The same happened during the reign of James V. After suffering a disastrous defeat in 1542, at the Battle of Solway Moss - a clash that resulted from the King's refusal to part from the Catholic Church - James V died, apparently from a "broken heart". His heir and successor? An infant daughter of six months, who would later become Mary, Queen of Scots. And just like that, Scotland was ruled by regents - not by a monarch. The child Mary was quickly sent abroad, to France, in order to protect her from the growing pressures by the English, whose King Henry VIII began a military campaign in order to forcefully marry the child Scottish Queen to his own son and heir, Edward. This period is known in history as the "Rough Wooing", also known as the Eight Years' War. Lasting from 1542 to 1551, it was mostly centered on the border regions between the two nations. In the end, the war proved a failure for the English, and only served to strengthen the alliance between Scotland and France at the time. However, during the increasingly pro-French politics of the Scottish regents, and the influx of French culture into Scotland, unpopularity for this foreign policy arose throughout the nation. This anti-French sentiment culminated in the Siege of Leith in 1560, where a contingent of French troops was stationed. The famed Treaty of Edinburgh was signed in that same year, which finally provided for the removal of French and English troops out of Scotland.

At the time, the Protestant Reformation already began to be felt in Scotland. It was a major movement within Western Christianity and was the biggest opponent of the Catholic Church and the Pope. The teaching of the first Protestant reformers, Martin Luther and John Calvin also reached the faraway regions of Scotland, and a reformation process began in earnest. Many Scottish scholars and priests that underwent education abroad, returned to Scotland and began spreading the influence and the teachings of the likes of John Calvin. During the process of the Scottish Reformation, many leading reformers and theologians were executed on accounts of heresy against the Catholic church. In 1528 one of the early Lutheran preachers, Patrick Hamilton, was executed in St. Andrews as a heretic. Just 18 years later, George Wishart died a martyr's death by being burned at the stake for his Protestant beliefs. However, these theologians were not alone in their cause: they had many Protestant supporters across Scotland, who were eager to get rid of Papal authority and the Catholic Church. In England, Protestantism took root before it did so in Scotland. During the period of the Eight Years' War (Rough Wooing), the English began supplying books and other Protestant material throughout the Lowlands, starting the spread of the teaching in Scotland. And the persecution of the Protestant adherents, especially the execution of Wishart, began to alienate the Scottish folk from the Catholic Church, and to grow even stronger in Protestant faith. The presence of the French in Scotland kept the Protestant cause suppressed - but as soon as the French were out of Scotland after the bringing of the Treaty of Edinburgh, Protestantism had space to flourish further.

One of the leading Scottish reformers was John Knox, who spent time studying under John Calvin in Geneva. Once he returned to Scotland, he spread his teachings and urged Scotsmen to reform their church in line with the teachings of Calvin. During the regency of Marie de Guise, the mother of Mary Queen of Scots, a period of political conflict emerged in Scotland, from which the Protestant party would eventually emerge victorious. In 1557, a group of Protestant lairds declared themselves the "Lords of Congregation" and were the party to represent Protestant interests. After Marie de Guise and the French were out of Scotland, the 1560 Scottish Reformation Parliament was formed and quickly abolished the authority of the former Catholic Church. A new Protestant church emerged in Scotland since then, organized after the Presbyterian traditions, and eventually formed the unique Church of Scotland, known also as the "Kirk".

Mary, Queen of Scots, returned to Scotland when she was 19. She was a Catholic but made no attempts to influence the faith of her Scottish subjects, who were now a majority of Protestants. But even so, her reign was short, lasting just six years, and full of instability, personal intrigues, and internal crisis. First of the scandals that shook her reign was the apparent murder of her second husband, Lord Darnley, who was a highly unpopular choice. The man's house in Edinburgh was obliterated by explosives, and his corpse found strangled in the garden. The number one suspect for the deed was the controversial Earl of Bothwell. In 1567, after several intrigues, Queen Mary was abducted by and married the Earl of Bothwell, a move that caused a great rift in Scottish society. An uprising quickly arose against the Queen and her new husband, and the conflict culminated in the Battle of Carberry Hill on June 15th, 1567. The Queen and her men were defeated: Earl Bothwell fled the scene, while Queen Mary was captured. She was then confined to the Lochleven Castle, where she was forced to abdicate the throne - in favor of her infant son, James VI. Mary did so, but soon escaped from her imprisonment and decided to continue her struggle for the throne. However, her attempts did not come to fruition: she - and the forces loyal to her - were defeated in 1568, at the Battle of Langside. Mary afterwards had to flee Scotland: she sought refuge in England, with her cousin Queen Elizabeth I. Meanwhile in Scotland, the supporters of Mary (known as the Queen's Men), fought a short but brutal civil war against the forces loyal to her infant son, King James VI (known as the King's Men). This period of instability was known as the Marian Civil War and lasted from 1568 to 1573. The war ended in favor of the King's Men. All the while, Mary was in England, but she never received the kind of support she wanted from her cousin, the queen. Instead, she became the focal point of several conspiracies and plots against Elizabeth I. These plots were orchestrated by ardent Catholics who were against the Protestant religion in England. Mary, as a Catholic monarch, was their ideal "candidate" for the English throne. These plots made attempts to oust Elizabeth and place Mary in her stead. In response, Elizabeth I had her cousin Mary imprisoned (with numerous liberties as is due to a monarch) for eighteen and a half years, an incredibly long time. In the end, the intrigues claimed Mary's life. She was found guilty of involvement in a plot to assassinate Elizabeth I and was executed by beheading on February 8th, 1587. She was 44 years old.

All the while, her young son James VI slowly ascended to the throne of Scotland. Until he came of age to rule in 1578, Scotland was left in charge of numerous regents. Even so, James' reign was the longest of any Scottish monarch, lasting 57 years and 246 days in total. During his reign, the aforementioned crucial event in Scottish history ensued: the Union of the Crowns, in 1603. When the English Queen Elizabeth I died childless, James VI came up as the only logical heir to the English throne, since he was the great-grandson of the ex-English King, Henry VII. With the Unification of the two crowns, he became James VI of Scotland and I of England, the monarch of "Great Britain and Ireland". However, both Scotland and England were independent sovereign states, each with its own laws, church, legislations and parliaments. However, they both had one King: James VI and I.

Did You Know?

One of the famed products of Scotland is undeniably its Scotch whisky. Known in Gaelic as "uisge beatha", the "water of life", it has a long and highly developed tradition in Scotland. The earliest *documented distilling of whisky dates to 1494, but evidence shows that it was well established by that time. However, interestingly enough, scholars think that whisky was introduced into Scotland from Ireland, where its distillation was known even before that point. Either way, it has become a foremost part of Scottish culture, cuisine, and heritage. Today, there are 134 whisky distilleries operating in Scotland, separated by distinct regions and different production methods. Whisky is made to a high standard and has to age in oak barrels for at least three years before sale. Did you know that archeologists managed to retrieve three cases of preserved Scotch whisky from the Antarctic ice that belonged to the doomed expedition of Ernest Shackleton? The whisky was bottled in 1898, and discovered in 2010, still extant. And did you know that the most expensive bottle of whisky ever sold was a bottle of Macallan Red Collection, sold at an auction for a whopping $975,756?*

Ever since the age of the reformation, the unbridgeable differences between the Protestants and the Catholics would mar the unfolding history of the British Isles. This yawning gap would intertwine itself into the reigns of many subsequent monarchs, following James VI, and would bring about some critical episodes in the histories of Ireland, Scotland, and England. Step by step, James VI and his successors attempted to join together the two independent Kingdoms which they ruled, England and Scotland. James initially made attempts to introduce parts of the English High Church Anglicanism in Scotland but had no tangible successes. His successor, Charles I Stuart, went as far as to introduce an English-styled prayer book into the Scottish Church, in 1637. He was quickly foiled in his attempts and had to face widespread riots across Scotland. In the following year, a national covenant was assembled, which attempted to limit the "liturgical innovations" of the King. As we can see, Protestantism took a solid root in Scotland, and no attempts to limit its spread were successful. In late 1638 the situation culminated when, at a meeting of the General

Assembly, the Scottish Bishops were formally expelled from the Kirk, which was then established on a Presbyterian basis. In response, King Charles I gathered his army, and Scotland was once more on the brink of bloodshed. However, a temporary solution was created in the form of the Pacification of Berwick. But just two years later, in 1640, the English troops of Charles I met in battle with the Covenanter troops loyal to the Scottish Kirk. It was the Battle of Newburn Ford, where the Scots won a valuable victory. These religious conflicts were collectively known as the Bishop's Wars, lasting for roughly a year, and were a part of the wider Wars of the Three Kingdoms, i.e., the British Civil Wars.

An Age of Differences and Bloodshed: Civil Wars

The Wars of the Three Kingdoms were a complex affair, involving the whole of the British Isles. It is a historic episode almost apart from the general history of Scotland, and as such it is a complex subject that is best explained in an entire book of its own. To that end, we shall not dwell on it all too much, and will only briefly address it in our History of Scotland.

Charles I was a central figure in the early British Civil Wars. He made attempts to pit the Irish Catholics against the Scottish Protestants and was met with fierce backlash and many revolts. When trying to deal with the Irish rebellion, Charles asked for additional funds from the English Parliament. Subsequent demands for a reform in England led to the English Civil War, a series of conflicts and clashes that involved Ireland, Scotland, and England collectively. The Scottish Covenanters played a major role in the conflict against Charles I and his religious policies and were the allies of the English Parliamentarians. Together, they won several victories in the civil war, notably at the Battle of Marston Moor. But not the whole of Scotland was united in its fight against its monarch Charles I. One Scotsman rose in arms against the Covenanters (who posed a majority in Scotland at the time) and made attempts to fight on the side of the King. This was James Graham, 1st Marquess of Montrose. Although he met little approval in the Scottish Highlands, he still managed to assemble a force of roughly a thousand Highlanders, Irishmen, and Islesmen to fight for King Charles. Graham led a surprisingly successful campaign across the Highlands, utilizing guerilla mobile warfare with incredible skill. He won some early victories, such as the Battle of Tippermuir in 1644, but suffered a crucial defeat in the Battle of Philiphaugh in 1645. Following his defeat at the Battle of Carbisdale in 1650, he was subsequently captured, tried, and executed by hanging and quartering. His head was on display in Edinburgh for eleven years.

In 1646, the civil war came to an end, and King Charles I was captured. His capture and subsequent trial were the culmination of the English Civil War and the raging conflict between the Parliamentarians and the Royalists. In early 1649, the victorious parliamentarian court declared Charles guilty of "uphold in himself an unlimited and tyrannical power to rule according to his will, and to overthrow the rights and liberties of the people", and subsequently sentenced him to death. Charles I Stuart was executed by beheading on January 30th, 1649. In subsequent decades, Charles was seen as a martyr.

Of course, the execution of Charles was met with much objection in Scotland, notably from the Covenanter party. Charles II, son of the executed Charles I, was quickly proclaimed King in Edinburgh. However, Oliver Cromwell, the most important figure of the English Civil War, would not let that sit idly, so he invaded Scotland in 1650. This led to the Anglo-Scottish War of 1650-1652. Cromwell at once scored a major victory over the Covenanters in the Battle of Dunbar, on September 3rd, 1650 - a crushing Scottish defeat. This was followed by another victory, this time in the Battle of Inverkeithing on July 20th, 1651. The new King, Charles II, not wanting to surrender, orchestrated an invasion into England, where he did not find sufficient support. Oliver Cromwell thus engaged them in battle, utterly defeating the Scottish Royalists in the Battle of Worcester, on September 3rd, 1651, exactly one year after his victory at Dunbar. Charles II managed to flee from the carnage. Subsequently, England occupied Scotland, and the latter was thus incorporated into its new Commonwealth. This meant the loss of its independent church government, of its own legal system and the parliament. This was the period of the so-called "Interregnum", lasting from 1649 to 1660. However, after the death of Oliver Cromwell, his short-lived regime largely collapsed. In 1660, Charles II was restored as the King of Scotland, England, and Ireland, and once more formally crowned in 1661. This move in many ways made the preceding 19 years null and void. With this, Scotland was once again independent, and regained its parliament, legal institutions, and the Kirk.

The Enduring Strife of the Highlands: Jacobitism

King Charles II died in 1685, and was succeeded by his brother, James VII of Scotland and II of England. However, James VII was a Roman Catholic, and quickly placed Catholics in all key positions within the government. This, however, alienated his Protestant subjects. Further instability and uncertainty arose when the question of an heir to the throne arose. James had no male heirs, and many firmly believed that he would be succeeded by his daughter, Mary II, and her Protestant husband, William of Orange, the Stadtholder of the Netherlands. However, James had a son born in 1688 - James Francis Edward Stuart. Realizing that the unpopular policies of James would likely continue with his son, the seven leading Englishmen created the so-called "Glorious Revolution", with which James VII and II was deposed. William of Orange entered England with 40,000 men, while James fled the throne, essentially "forfeiting the crown". In the end, William of Orange and his wife Mary II became the new King and Queen. William was succeeded by Queen Anne, the younger daughter of James. She would be the last British monarch from the House of Stuart.

William of Orange had plenty of supporters, and his reign was somewhat tolerant. However, there were still a lot of supporters for the cause of the exiled James VII. A significant following for his cause arose in the Scottish Highlands, and his supporters became known as "Jacobites" (from Jacobus, Latin for James). Jacobitism led to a series of uprisings in the Scottish Highlands, with the attempt to reinstate Stuarts to the throne. The first of these uprisings arose in 1689.

At this moment, it is important to understand the complexities of the Jacobite movement and of the Jacobite causes. Jacobites were composed of both Protestant Lowlanders, and Catholic Highlanders, even though James was a Catholic King. By the mid-1700s, less than 1% of all Scotsmen were Catholics, and that faith was upheld only in the far north, amongst a few noble families and commoners. In general, the cause was full of contradictions. But even so, there were four major Jacobite uprisings: in 1689, 1715, 1719, and 1745.

In 1689, the First Jacobite rising saw many Highlanders rise up in revolt, led by the "Bonnie Dundee" - John Graham of Claverhouse, 1st Viscount Dundee. In this uprising, the Jacobites fought the Williamite forces of Hugh Mackay, and initially won a major victory in the Battle of Killiecrankie, on July 27th 1689. It was Bonnie Dundee's greatest victory - however it was also his last. He died in the fighting, and the loss of such a competent leader also meant that the First Jacobite Uprising would be a short-lived affair. Major clashes ended in 1690, but the conflict endured in the Highlands until 1692. The first uprising ended in a tragic way, with the infamous Massacre of Glencoe which occurred on February 13th, 1692. In this event, the English massacred some 38 members of Clan MacDonald, allegedly for their failure to swear allegiance to William and Mary II. The truth was, that the Jacobite chiefs of the highland clans agreed to swear loyalty to them as early as 1690, but never did so. The massacre shocked the public at the time.

Did You Know?

Rob Roy MacGregor is one of Scotland's most loved folk heroes. Born in 1671 as Raibeart Ruadh MacGriogair and grew up to be an influential figure in the Jacobite risings of the Highland clans. After the failure of Bonnie Dundee's first Jacobite Uprising in 1689, Rob Roy eventually became a cattleman, operating a Highland Watch over the herds of the Landed Gentry. In essence, it was an extortion racket, commonplace throughout the Highlands at the time. Through this lifestyle, Rob Roy borrowed a great deal of money to expand his own cattle herds, but later defaulted on his loan. This placed him in direct conflict with his creditor, the powerful James Graham, 1st Duke of Montrose, who seized Rob Roy's lands in retaliation. A fierce blood feud was born out of this, with Rob Roy becoming an outlaw, seeking vengeance against the noble Duke of Montrose. Rob Roy's highland adventures were romanticized in the decades after his death in 1734, and he became a Highland folk hero, a daring outlaw. With the release of the novel "Rob Roy" in 1817, which was written by Sir Walter Scott, his adventures became widely popular across the world, not just in Scotland.

In the early 1700s, the Union of Scotland and England was becoming a promising idea that would benefit the British Isles both economically and politically. For Scotland especially, this idea seemed particularly attractive since it suffered from intense economic stagnation. Its economy depended on its trade with England, and increased pressures for the Union made it an all the more possible outcome. We must understand that much of Scotland was a poor, rural, and agriculture-focused society, with just 1.3 million inhabitants in the mid-1700s. Thus, the idea of uniting with the much more prosperous England was a very attractive idea at the time. And so it was that on January 6th, 1707, the Scottish Parliament voted in favor of adopting the Treaty of Union. This led to the creation of Great Britain, and in the end - benefited Scotland on an incredible level. It was later said that "by the union with England, the middling and inferior ranks of people in Scotland gained a complete deliverance from the power of an aristocracy which had always before oppressed them." And thanks to the integration into England's bustling imperial economy, Scotland could at last get out of the shadow of the aristocracy, and to bloom into a modernized, bountiful, and forward-facing society. Furthermore, the Union replaced the Scottish currency, trade laws, and taxation, but left the Scottish Church unchanged and unaffected, and its own law also. For the first time in centuries, Scotland could enjoy the prospects of a bright and prosperous future. However, the path towards success was not smooth: there were yet a few conflicts in store before peace and prosperity could arrive.

These conflicts pertain to the Jacobite cause, as we mentioned before. In 1715, a new uprising surfaced, known popularly as the "Fifteen". It was an attempt by James Francis Edward Stuart, the so-called "Old Pretender" to reclaim the English, Scottish, and Irish throne and restore the Stuart dynasty. He was the son and heir of James VII and II. Once again, the Jacobite flag was unfurled in the Highlands, and many clans and chieftains flocked to the cause. The uprising lasted only a year and was ultimately a failure. James Stuart arrived from exile, and entered Scotland on December 22nd, 1715, but again departed on January 30th, 1716.

In 1719, the third Jacobite Uprising broke out, as a renewed attempt by the Old Pretender to regain his throne. This revolt ended in the same year in which it began and was disastrous from the get-go. Its outcome would severely damage the overall Stuart cause and their supporters. The so-called "Nineteen" was the only Jacobite uprising to involve the forces of Spain, who were at the time at war with England. However, with their fleet damaged by stormy seas, the Spanish could not come through with their intended plans. The Third Jacobite Uprising ended with a disastrous defeat at the Battle of Glen Shiel on June 10th, 1719. Involved were men of Clans Cameron, MacGregor, MacKenzie, Murray, Keith, and MacKinnon.

The fourth, and last Jacobite Uprising occurred in 1745, known then as the "Forty-Five". This was an attempt by the son of the Old Pretender, Charles Edward Stuart, to regain the throne for his own father. Charles was known in the Highlands as Bonnie Prince Charlie. The Jacobite flag once more arose, this time in Glenfinnan in the Highlands - several highland clans joined the cause of Bonnie Prince Charlie. In stark contrast to the previous uprising, the '45 was marked with initial success. The forces of Bonnie Prince Charlie succeeded in capturing Edinburgh and won a decisive victory against the government forces at the Battle of Prestonpans, on September 21st, 1745. It was a fantastic win: the battle lasted just 30 minutes, as the government troops broke and fled when witnessing a ferocious Highland charge. This was followed up by another victory, this time on January 17th, 1746, at the Battle of Falkirk Muir.

The Jacobites managed to penetrate into England, where they hoped to receive the aid of English Jacobites. They took Carlisle and penetrated southward, reaching Derby. However, they began to doubt this endeavor, as it was clear that a Catholic Stuart monarch would never receive support in England. Fearing that their retreat routes would be cut off, and with encroaching English armies, the Jacobite forces began to retreat back into Scotland. Once back, a string of failures began to slowly crumble the '45 uprising. Edinburgh was lost, and an attempt to take Stirling failed. The tattered Jacobite army began to retreat further inland, towards Inverness, with the Government forces hot at their heels. Bonnie Prince Charlie was at last caught up at Culloden, where a fierce battle took place on April 16th, 1746.

Culloden was the great tragedy of the Highlands: many Clans suffered immense casualties in this battle. It was the ultimate defeat for the Jacobites: the battle lasted just an hour, and the Jacobite forces suffered around 2,000 casualties, compared to just 300 on the Government side. Amongst the chief clans that were at Culloden were Clans Grant, Gunn, MacKenzie, Ross, MacKay, Sutherland, Fraser, and many others. Bonnie Prince Charlie fled to the Hebrides, where he was constantly pursued by the government forces. With the help of loyal clans, he made his way to Skye, from where he departed to France, never again to return to Scotland. Culloden marked the end of the Jacobite cause, and also the end of the romanticized, heroic era of Highlander Clans.

Following the failure and the end of the Jacobite cause, severe reprisals occurred across the Highlands, as the government forces made attempts to root out Jacobitism once and for all. The Old Pretender died in 1760 without ever achieving his goals, and his son, Bonnie Prince Charlie, died in 1788 - without a legitimate heir. The Jacobite era thus truly ended. One only has to wonder and ask the question: was all the death and suffering worth it? The noble Scottish Highlands were scarred so badly during the four Jacobite risings - the Clans suffered, and young men fought and died so that wealthy monarchs could continue to rule over them and reap the benefits.

The Emergence of a Modern, Recovering Scotland:
Post-Jacobite Era

Perhaps, the blood had to be lost so that Scotland could at last enter into the limelight of the modern, prosperous contemporary world. As the Jacobite cause collapsed, ceasing disruptions to progress, and the Union with England came to fruition, Scotland was able to experience a fresh start, a chance at prosperity. A stable middle class emerged in Scotland, and new career opportunities surfaced for many Scots. The Lowlanders were amongst the first to reap the rewards of these new opportunities: many sought their new beginnings in politics, the army, the navy, economy, trade, and civil service. Others found their success in the endeavors of the British Empire as a whole, emigrating across the seas to the New World - the Americas. In fact, thousands upon thousands of Scots sought a new beginning across the seas, leaving their Highland homes forever. Around this time, however, the last remnants of an archaic, traditional Scotland would inevitably crumble before the onset of the modern, prosperous era into which Scotland was entering with big, bold steps. And that archaic element was the Highland Clan system. This traditional, patriarchal, and feudal society was a big challenge for the rulers of Scotland and for the government. Simply because they were firmly rooted in their traditional way of life and hard to govern. Many attempts were made to integrate the Clans and the Highlands into Scottish society.

However, the Clans themselves changed across the centuries. By the 18th century, Clan chiefs were in many ways separate from their clansmen, and were akin to commercial landlords and nobles, instead of clansmen who would lead their people. Rents were a commonplace thing across the Highlands - either in goods or money. This meant that all tenants living on a laird's land had to pay rents. This was often a difficult thing for the poor, rural communities of the remote highlands. However, with this change of "lifestyles" amongst the clan leaders, they began to accumulate large debts. Many clan leaders were thus "forced" to sell their Highland estates. With the creation of the Heritable Jurisdictions Act of 1746, the judicial roles of clan chiefs were removed, and transferred to the Scottish courts. Further to deteriorate the Highland Clan system was the new agricultural improvement that was introduced in the late 1700s. However, these improvements were followed with numerous evictions which were known collectively as Highland Clearances. Together with these clearances, as well as the 1846 Highland potato famine, increased emigration from the Highlands left them increasingly depopulated. People emigrated from the Highlands all the way until the Great Depression before the Second World War. Many Scots found their new beginnings in Australia, America, England, or Mainland Europe.

From all this, however, Scotland emerged as a new, reformed, and successful nation. It was the beginning of a wholly new era - one of success, prosperity, and enlightenment. In fact, its rise to prosperity was so abrupt that many were surprised by it. In the 18th and 19th centuries, education bloomed, and new intellectual and scientific achievements originated in this nation. The major cities bloomed, and a network of universities, schools, libraries, and museums spread through Scotland. In many ways, this was the chance that was needed - a chance for the Scots to show to the world their abilities and their considerable contributions to the great progress of the World as a whole. Some of the leading Scots to emerge in the Enlightenment period were noted philosophers, painters, writers and poets, architects, inventors, mathematicians and scientists, soldiers and noted generals, historians, botanists, sailors and astronomers. From an age of turmoil and bloodshed, Scotland emerged anew and full of ambition. Arthur Herman, in his work called "How the Scots Invented the Modern World" sums it up nicely:

"Scottish Whigs had helped to defeat Jacobitism in order to give birth to a new enlightened Scotland. They got their wish - with a vengeance. The years after 1745 witnessed an explosion of cultural and economic activity all across Scotland, as if the collapse of the Jacobite and Highland threat had released a tremendous pent-up store of national energy. It was an economic "takeoff" in the full modern sense."

The Age of Enlightenment:
Scotland's New Start

In many ways, if it weren't for the Scottish people, and the flow of the history of their nation, the world as we know it today would not be the same. Great names arose in that enlightenment era - great names eager to reshape the future of the world. Some of these were: Henry Bell (1767–1830) engineer who introduced the first passenger steamboat service in Europe; Joseph Black (1728–1799), a physicist and chemist, the first man to isolate carbon dioxide; Robert Burns (1759–1796), the most celebrated and iconic Scottish poet; Thomas Carlyle (1795–1881), a noted historian, essayist and philosopher; Adam Ferguson (1723–1816), a leading philosopher who is considered the founder of sociology; Matthew Hardie (1755–1826), a famed violin maker who was called the "Scottish Stradivari"; Francis Home (1719–1813) a successful physician and first to make attempts at vaccination against measles; David Hume (1711–1776) a philosopher, historian and essayist who introduced an immensely influential system of philosophical empiricism, skepticism, and naturalism; James Hutton (1726–1797) a geologists and founder of modern geology; Sir Alexander Mackenzie (1764–1820), an explorer of North America and the first to complete the east to west crossing of America; Thomas Reid (1710–1796), a philosopher and founder of the Scottish School of Common Sense; Sir Walter Scott (1771–1832), one of the most famous Scottish novelists, known for his works such as Ivanhoe, Rob Roy, Waverley, and others; Sir John Ross (1777–1856), a noted Arctic explorer - and many, many others.

From the mid 1700's and onwards, Scotland's industrial and economic rise was apparent. While many parts of the nation were still impoverished and poor - such as the Highlands and the Isles as we mentioned - the rest steadily marched on to prosperity. Glasgow and

Edinburgh arose as dominant industrial and economic centers, specializing in many different trades. Scotsmen benefited from trade with America, exporting there heavily. However, the outbreak of the American Revolutionary War put an end to that, due to the blockading of ports. Nevertheless, Glasgow emerged as a major industrial center in the British Isles. Scotland was investing in textiles, iron, glass, soap work, alcohol, rope, and sugar. In time, linen formed the foundation of Scotland's industry in the 18th century. From linen, this expanded to jute, cotton, and wool. One great fact that contributed to the success of the Scottish economy at the time was a special industrial policy that was made up by the *"board of trustees for Fisheries and Manufactures in Scotland"*. Their goal was to create an economy that would be *complementary*, and not *competitive* with England. That way the two leading economies of the United Kingdom could benefit one from another, furthering the success. In time, Scotland became one of the leading world exporters of linen. In fact, the British Linen Company that was established in 1746, became the largest such firm of the 18th century, exporting its goods all over, especially to America.

Industry was not the only thing to bloom in Scotland at that time. Spurred onwards by the rise of education, literature also flourished - in a distinct Scottish way. The development of Scottish literature in the age of Enlightenment was a key component of the forming of a strong Scottish national identity. Even though the Scottish Gaelic language was largely replaced by English and the distinct Scots, the Scottish people still found ways to express their national ideas and traditions through the written word. The likes of Sir Walter Scott would become one of the famed novelists of the world, not just Scotland. Scott, of Clan Scott heritage, would go on to write the classics of world literature, such as *Waverley* in 1814, *Rob Roy* in 1817, *Ivanhoe* in 1820, and many, many others. His works are adored even today.

Poetry equally bloomed in Scotland. One of the earliest poets was Allan Ramsay (1686-1758), who helped rekindle the interest in the old Scottish literature and contributed immensely to the emergence of a unique Scottish poetic form. Following him was James MacPherson, who helped translate the classic Ossian cycle which would go on to acquire international popularity. The work spread throughout Europe to universal acclaim and went on to inspire the European great authors such as Goethe and Herder. Of course, arguably the most famous Scottish poet was Robert Burns (1759-1796). The eldest son of an unsuccessful tenant farmer from Ayrshire, Burns grew up in poverty and demanding manual labor. He was acutely aware of his "social disadvantage" and began to write poetry as an escape from the harsh realities of low class Scottish life. He wrote in his native *Scots* language, which helped to introduce poetry to a wider audience and rural Scotsmen who could read Scots and connect it with their own identity. When he was on the brink of emigrating from Scotland, due to a broken heart, Burns published his *"Poems; Chiefly in the Scottish Dialect"* - a collection of poems which was met with incredible acclaim and was an immense success. He became a major figure in the Romantic movement, and helped collect many traditional Scottish folk songs, preserving them for posterity. He is considered as the national poet of Scotland and one of its iconic cultural symbols. His poem "Auld Lang Syne" is still widely popular across Scotland and sung on Hogmanay. Another one of his poems, "Scots Wha Hae" was for a long time the unofficial national anthem of Scotland.

Did You Know?

The Loch Ness monster is one of the most enduring myths of Scotland. Loch Ness is a large freshwater loch situated in the Scottish Highlands, near Inverness. Overlooked by the picturesque Urquhart Castle, the loch is said to be the home of a cryptozoological water beast, a "long extinct plesiosaurus", named Nessie. Some say that the earliest reported sighting of a mysterious water beast is traced to the times of Saint Columba. More recent sightings of a beast began in 1871, then in 1888, when one Alexander MacDonald reported seeing an enormous "salamander-like" beast exiting the loch. The reports continued to mount, and an enduring myth of some prehistoric beast that roamed the loch was firmly rooted in Scottish folklore. Curiously, Loch Ness is exceptionally deep, and there are locals who are firmly convinced that such a beast exists, "beyond any doubt". Numerous expeditions were conducted over the years, hoping to sight or even catch the prehistoric creature, but no considerable success was ever made. Nessie remains one of the mysteries of the Highlands.

Of course, a blooming literature could not be achieved without proper education. The roots of modern education in Scotland lie in the Reformation, which aimed for schools in every parish. In later decades, landowners were obliged to provide a schoolhouse in rural communities, and to pay for schoolmasters, helping increase literacy and education. Furthermore, the religious headmasters in these parishes were often educated at universities and helped with the quality of education in schoolhouses. Alas, the schools in Scotland taught in the English language, which further deteriorated the survival of Scottish Gaelic. By the 18th century, Scotland was one of the regional leaders when it came to education and boasted the whole of five universities: in Glasgow, St. Andrews, Edinburgh, and two in Aberdeen. In comparison, England had only two universities. These universities were originally centered on legal and clerical education. But after the events of the 17th century this was broadened immensely, and students were now able to get educated in spheres of economics and science. Ultimately, universities of Scotland became leading centers for medical education, which helped place Scotland at the very forefront of the Enlightenment movement. All this helped produce some great minds in Scotland: scientists, inventors, writers, and philosophers - true heroes of education that arose from a scarred and tumultuous Scotland of the 17th century. Many doubted this nation and its potential. In the centuries before this, the English considered Scots as brutes who cling to an archaic and primitive Highland way of life. However, the Scots were far, far more than this. They were a people of great romantic notion, a freedom-loving people who were as free and beautiful and wild at heart as the rugged nature around them. A people who stayed firmly by their beliefs and convictions, persevering through the ages in order to finally come out on top and prove to the world their capabilities and eloquence.

In the 19th century, Scotland's successes continued to mount steadily. Its rise to prosperity was surprising to many, as its apparent transformation into a bountiful leader of the region's modern industry came somewhat suddenly. And it wasn't just the economy and industry that were on the rise - the demographics were equally booming. The populace of Scotland increased nearly trifold in the course of just a century. In 1801, the census showed that there were just 1,608,000 inhabitants in the nation. In 1851 this count rose to 2,889,000, and in 1901 to an incredible 4,472,000. In comparison, the population count of Scotland in 2019 was roughly 5,500,000. These counts tell us that the prosperity that Scotland enjoyed in its enlightenment era made it a good nation to live in, and that despite the slow crumble of its old traditions and lifestyles, and despite the high emigration to overseas colonies, life nonetheless bloomed in the nation. Of course, throughout the course of Scottish history, the population count rarely exceeded 2 million. This new, increased population count that soared to nearly 5 million in the late 1800s meant that new villages and towns sprouted throughout the nation. Regions that were previously sparsely populated were now bustling with life. Furthermore, cities grew in size, becoming the first true metropolises in Scotland. The sudden change from a rural, agriculture-based society into one of industry and mass production meant that more and more people flocked to the cities and the Lowlands in search of work and prosperity. In the west of the country, in the Highlands and the Hebrides, sheep farming and commercial fishing became lucrative enterprises. This helped the rise of the cotton weaving industry, in which Scotland was one of the global leaders. This, however, abruptly ended with the outbreak of the American Civil War in the mid-1800s. Nevertheless, Scotland's economy did not suffer. It was still a leading producer of linen and had almost inexhaustible sources of coal. Thanks to this it became a world leader in the shipbuilding industry (being surrounded by ocean, after all), of engineering, and the locomotive industry. Some of Scotland's leading railway engineers were hired across the world where they began introducing modernized railway systems. All of this helped cement Scotland's position in the world, transforming it from an impoverished country with a troubled history, into a leading industrial center and a modern sovereign nation with a proud and rich national heritage.

Prominent Scots bloomed in their homeland, but also spread their achievements to other parts of the world. Some Scots that emigrated from their homes became the most successful men and women in global history. Examples include Andrew Carnegie, who left Scotland with his parents at age 12, and became one of the leading entrepreneurs and businessmen in the United States, leading the expansion of the American steel industry and becoming one of the richest men in history of that nation. He was also a philanthropist, donating millions upon millions of dollars to charities and universities, seeking to improve society through his wealth. Another prominent emigree Scotsman was Alexander Graham Bell, a famed inventor who is credited with patenting the first practical telephone. Born in Edinburgh, he became based in America as one of the leading inventors of his time. He co-founded the American Telephone and Telegraph Company, the renowned AT&T. These men and their achievements - and those of many other Scots - leave us greatly indebted today to Scotland, to whose sons and daughters we have a lot to thank for.

Modern Scotland

As a part of the United Kingdom, Scotland was unavoidably involved with the First World War, which ravaged the world in the early 20th century. A giant of the UK's industry, Scotland was an important aspect of the British war effort. First and foremost, Scotland provided the war effort with manpower. Scottish soldiers were praised and renowned in Britain's army, known for their resilience, bravery, and daring feats. Many Highlanders coming from poor crofting families sought their fortunes in military service, where they became exceptionally regarded. But besides manpower, Scotland also provided the war effort with funds, ships, machinery, and fish. A notable example of just in what measure Scotland's industry helped the war effort comes from the archives of the Singer Clydebank sewing machine factory. During the war years, this factory produced an incredible 303 million artillery shells, and shell components, as well as additional rifles, grenades, and airplane parts. Records also state that some 690,000 Scottish soldiers were sent to Europe into combat, where 74,000 gave their lives in battle and to disease, while 150,000 were seriously wounded. Of these men, many came from the more impoverished areas of Scotland, especially after 1916, with the introduction of recruitment. For example, sparsely populated areas, such as the isle of Lewis and Harris in the Hebrides, was left almost depopulated due to unproportional losses it suffered. Even those that did not fight in Europe did their part for the war effort. Shipyards of Scotland, such as the ones at Clydeside, were busily producing the equipment for the war effort. The Great War was a terrible era of global history, and these numbers tell us just how big a sacrifice Scotland made in that conflict. And that sacrifice needs to be remembered.

Alas, war rarely leads to a positive outcome. Even though the Allies were victorious in the Great War, the United Kingdom was greatly affected. It gave an enormous push, and nearly pushed itself over the edge - which greatly affected its economy. Even though Scotland's shipbuilding industry continued to bloom in the postwar years, the economic depression that raged through Britain and the rest of Europe was soon to affect the Scottish economy as well. By 1922, the depression was prominently felt in Scotland. The nation's specialized heavy industry was hit hard, and its workers found it difficult to find suitable employment elsewhere. This led to a great economic stagnation in Scotland, a stark contrast to the industrial boom it enjoyed in the preceding decades. Unemployment became rampant in Scotland (as elsewhere in Europe), which led to poor housing, social issues, poor health, and a general national descent into poverty. One of the few Scottish industries that did manage to bloom during this time was whisky production: Scottish whisky, the so-called "Scotch", was sought after worldwide, especially in the United States, even during its Prohibition era. Yet even so, the booming whisky industry was not enough to lead Scotland out of its economic stagnation. This general poverty once again led to a wave of emigration to overseas countries. Records show that an estimated 400,000 Scots left their homeland between 1921 and 1931 - an incredibly high number for such a short time span. During this time, Scots who were affected by poverty were attracted by better job opportunities in America (for example), where many had cousins and families to go to. The most common destinations for emigrating Scots were America, Canada, and Australia. However, this rampant wave of Scottish emigration was quickly halted with the onset of the Great Depression in America that began in the 1930s, ending the opportunities and prosperity in that country.

Did You Know?

St. Kilda is one of Scotland's most remote places. An archipelago far to the west of the Outer Hebrides, St. Kilda has long been an object of fascination for many historians, travelers, and researchers. Its main island, Hirta, has been inhabited for centuries, even though it was so remote. Possessing only a single village, Hirta and its inhabitants developed a set of unique practices and a lifestyle that was modeled on their incredible isolation. In fact, these islanders were so isolated, that many of them died once exposed to smallpox and other diseases from traveling ships. Today, the island is uninhabited. The archipelago is home to three additional islands - Dun, Soay and Boreray - as well as several prominent sea stacks. These islands are home to very rare species of sheep, only extant here. On the whole, St. Kilda archipelago is very enigmatic, having a unique history that was shaped by and large by its remoteness.

Following the turbulent and economically difficult 1930s, the Second World War broke out, pushing the world into a new global conflict that would claim millions of lives. Just as in the Great War, Scotland became an important part of the British war effort. Glasgow and Clydeside shipyards were a big part of the overall war effort, working around the clock to bolster the British war machine. In the Scottish islands of Orkney, the naval base of Scapa Flow played a major role in the war, being the home of a crucial Royal Navy base. The Axis forces were quick to lead attacks on Scapa Flow, and the location was the site of some decisive aerial clashes. The reach of the Axis bombers extended into mainland Scotland also, as the shipyards of Glasgow were heavily bombarded by Germany's Luftwaffe.

The Shetland Islands also played a key role in the war, mainly due to their proximity to Norway - which was under German occupation. Overall, in the Battle for the North Atlantic, Scotland and its outlying islands played a key role. Of course, just as in the Great War, many young Scotsmen went to fight in many of the global theaters of war. A part of the British Army, Scotsmen fought in France, Belgium, Holland, and Germany, in Italy and North Africa, as well as in the Far East. Again, they were noted for their bravery, their achievements, and that unmistakable Scottish highlander spirit. But sadly, as in the previous conflict, casualties that Scotland's brave sons sustained were appallingly high.

Nevertheless, Scotland came out of the Second World War with its head held up high, proud and battle-scarred. Once again, its industry managed to soar high, to overcome difficulties and to help Scotland as a whole to get back up on its feet. The shipbuilding industry never faltered and was now at the height of its productivity. Other heavy industries that were involved in military business and helped produce heavy machines, tanks, and guns, also prospered. This helped greatly reduce unemployment, rendering it virtually nonexistent in the postwar years. Besides the heavy industry, agriculture prospered as well, supporting the more rural parts of the nation and keeping sheep and cattle farming in a steady rise. Wages were increased dramatically, attracting new workers in all spheres of Scotland's industry. This all led to an improved housing situation, to increased birth rates, better quality of food, and in general - a much better quality of life for all Scots. In a dramatic turn of events, Scotland emerged from the horrors of war with a renewed ambition, ready to tackle the period of reconstruction and healing with unshakable confidence. In a true Highlander spirit, this proud nation bent its back and worked very hard, healing the scars of history - one step at a time.

In modern times, Scotland is a prosperous, modern nation and a key part of the United Kingdom. However, there are increased calls for independence in recent times, a crucial topic in Scottish society that has been present throughout its history. Ever since the Union of the two Crowns, some Scots still held on to the idea of a sovereign, fully independent Scotland. This call for independence culminated in recent times, resulting in the 2014 Scottish Independence Referendum. The referendum asked citizens a simple question: "Should Scotland be an independent country?" A total of 2,001,926 Scottish voters voted

"No", compared to 1,617,989 who voted "Yes". Even though the results were clear, the question still exists as a burning topic in modern Scotland. After all, a great part of Scotland's history is based on a centuries-long struggle for freedom, with many bloody battles dotting the pages of its history. A strong desire for independence is thus rooted in Scottish DNA, in many ways. The question of the nation's independence is thus not yet resolved, although for the time being, it remains an invaluable part of the UK.

Conclusion

Out of all this, the modern nation of Scotland as we know it, emerged. This is a nation of unique heritage, a special Gaelic-Pictish identity that miraculously persevered through the many centuries of struggle. And it is this unique "parentage" of the Scottish people that gives them that zest for natural, exciting, and fulfilled life. The Scottish nation is a nation of fighters, of highlanders who breathe in life with full lungs, with appreciation and joy. This is a nation of freedom-loving people above all: century after century, the Scots fought to preserve their independence and to cast away the shackles of English intruders. Fierce people, with the romantic traditions of the Gaels, and the fighting spirit of the Picts, they remained true to themselves, always wary of the "Sassenachs" in their lands. Theirs is a history of war and injustice, and oppression. But from their history we can understand that patience and perseverance, and the preservation of a true cause, will lead a nation to the freedom it sought for so long.

From the murky prehistory to the conflicts of the Gaels and Picts, down to the arrival of the Norse and the meddling of the English and the Normans - the nation of Scotland was ever the crossroads of nations and cultures. And rare are such crossroads where the meeting parties can co-exist and live together in peace. Rare indeed: in fact, they often end in bloodshed and warfare. Scotland is a crucial example of one such cultural crossroad, where waves of arriving cultures scarred the land with their axes, swords, muskets, and guns. And through all that, the proud Scots endured. It is to these hardy people that we must look, realizing their struggle and their harsh, harsh lifestyle in the remote glens, the faraway islands, and the windswept highlands. It is an enormous struggle, generations of hardy folk that had to live with loss and sacrifice. Men dying in battles, women fleeing with their children, sons avenging their fathers. And as we know, it is the hard times that create hard men and women. And Scotland's men and women indeed are hard and enduring, shaped through the centuries of their forebears' struggle.

After all is said and done, Scotland is a nation to be admired - a nation whose histories can be studied over and over in order to understand what it truly means to be *free*.

References:

Bambery, C. 2014. *A People's History of Scotland.* Verso Books.

Brown, P. H. 1911. *History of Scotland to the Present Time.* CUP Archive.

Devine, T. M. and Wormald, J. 2012. *The Oxford Handbook of Modern Scottish History.* OUP Oxford.

Hubbard, H. 2020. *History of Scotland.* Richmont.

Lang, A. 2006. *Scottish History in 33 Chapters.* Scotlandview.

Lang, A. 2012. *A Short History of Scotland.* Tredition.

Lang, A. *The History Of Scotland – Volume 1: From The Romans to Mary of Guise.* Jazzybee Verlag.

Mackie, J. D. 2013. *Scottish History.* Cambridge University Press.

Robertson, W. 1806. *The History of Scotland During the Reigns of Queen Mary and of King James VI.* T. Cadell and W. Davis.

Santiuste, D. 2015. *The Hammer of the Scots: Edward I and the Scottish Wars of Independence.* Pen and Sword.

Unknown. 2021. *Scottish History: by History-Episode - Fascinating History of Scotland From Beginning to the End.* BookSummaryGr.

Wormald, J. 2011. *Scotland: A History.* Oxford University Press.

Don't miss out!

Visit the website below and you can sign up to receive emails whenever History Nerds publishes a new book. There's no charge and no obligation.

https://books2read.com/r/B-A-ODOK-PTFXB

Connecting independent readers to independent writers.

Also by History Nerds

Celtic History
Ireland

Great Wars of the World
World War 1
World War 2
The Napoleonic Wars: One Shot at Glory
The Serbian Revolution: 1804-1835
Peace Won by the Saber: The Crimean War, 1853-1856
The Wars of the Roses

Irish Heroes
Grace O'Malley: The Pirate Queen of Ireland
William Butler Yeats: Nobel Prize Winning Poet
Scáthach
Finn McCool

The History of the Vikings

Vikings
Longships on Restless Seas

The Rise and Fall of Empires
Rome: The Rise and Fall

Standalone
The History of the United Kingdom
The History of Ireland
The History of America
Stalin
The Fiery Maelstrom of Freedom
The History of Scotland
Robert the Bruce
William Wallace: Scotland's Great Freedom Fighter
The History of Wales